Navigate
Chaos

A 5-Step Guide
to Balance Work,
Family, and Other
Life Priorities

Steven B. Wiley

Printed in the United States of America

ISBN: 978-1-7325176-0-8
Library of Congress Control Number: 2018909208

Cover design by Whitley Carson

For more information, visit www.ceekllc.com.

For bulk book orders, contact info@ceekllc.com.

Note to the Reader

In an effort to provide relevant stories from my life, this book makes several references to faith and God. For the record, I'm a Christian who's comfortable sharing my beliefs as well as my doubts, fears, and insecurities. While my faith has provided a strong foundation that has helped in my pursuit of healthy life balance, I acknowledge that there are many other religions and belief systems that have done, and can do, the same for others. Regardless of your faith or beliefs, foundational values and a strong character are instrumental in anyone's pursuit of healthy life balance. As emphasized throughout this book, you are encouraged to consider the relevance of your own belief system, priorities, and values as you contemplate the guidance and recommendations offered.

The advice and strategies in this book may not be suitable for every situation. This book is sold with the understanding that neither the author nor the publisher is held responsible for results, or the lack of, based on the advice in this book. Specifically, neither the author nor the publisher makes any warranties or guarantees about any of the content or recommendations in this book. Readers are cautioned to rely on their own judgment about their individual circumstances and to act accordingly.

This book is dedicated to my wife and children. You are and will always be the priority in my life. I thank you for your unconditional love, understanding, and patience as I learned to *Navigate Chaos* in pursuit of a healthy and balanced life.

Table of Contents

Foreword

Written by Kristine Sisson
Former colleague and now friend of the author

I really didn't like Steve Wiley when I met him.

I was working sixty- to eighty-hour weeks for a consulting company in Virginia. In my mind, I had it all—a house, a career, and a dog. I was good at my job as a project manager and gave everything I had to my client, project, and team. I hadn't taken a vacation in more than two years. I took my laptop to bed with me when I was sick. After I got home and took the dog for a quick walk, I'd log back in again. It wasn't sustainable or realistic. As far as I knew, I was happy; this was the life I wanted.

Steve took it away.

When Steve came on as an account manager, he began to evaluate all the teams in his area. Around that time, my project's client had reported some problems. Even though I wasn't the source of the issues, Steve decided that I needed a change and so did the project. While working to resolve the client's concerns, he took me off the project and pulled me from the team I loved.

Steve understood that my approach to work and life wasn't sustainable. I now know that he was concerned about me personally and professionally, but at the time I didn't care because I was angry. My client was angry. Steve knew it was a potential risk to pull me from the contract, but he held his ground and started looking for a new project for me. I started looking for a new job outside of the company. I didn't want to talk to Steve or see his face. I even kept my office door shut all day; I was that hurt and angry.

Steve committed to finding me a new opportunity within the company, but I didn't believe him. While I was looking for a new job, Steve placed me with a different team within the company. I knew nothing about the team, and I felt alone. I found out much later that this team worked with one of the most demanding clients Steve had ever encountered. He thought I would be a good fit for the client, but, more importantly, that the team and the client understood the value of balance and built it into its culture. He believed I could not only be successful professionally on that team but that I could also create a more sustainable, balanced way of working for myself.

Months later, I was still upset, but I remember hearing Steve talk about balance at the quarterly team meetings and thinking, "Okay, I think I get it." I started trying to incorporate balance into my life. It wasn't easy. I continued to work hard at my job, but I had learned that taking time for myself was good for me personally and professionally. It took me six months to get used to this change, but I now had time for other things. I took my dog for walks after work—leisurely ones, since I didn't have to log back in to work. I took my nieces to the park and worked on my house. I started enjoying the simple things that most people take for granted but that I hadn't done in such a long time.

About that time, Shane, a friend I grew up with who now lived in Arizona, reached out to me. After talking on the phone, I decided to fly out to visit him. I would never have been able to do that before. There wouldn't have been time.

Now I had time. I had the flexibility to work remotely, flying back and forth to Arizona to see Shane and his two beautiful sons. For the first time in a long time, something other than work was important to me. I saw what it was to work, have a life, and embrace a family.

Eventually, I became a full-time teleworker after moving to Arizona. Shane and I married, and we had a son. It all worked because I was practicing balance and worked on a team with an account manager who was committed to the same philosophy.

And just when we thought we had it all figured out, life threw us a huge curveball.

My husband got sick with terminal cancer. Without my practice and my team's commitment to balance, I wouldn't have been able to continue to work, be with my husband during treatment, and care for our three-year-old. I don't know what I would have done otherwise. I needed to work: practically because we needed the health insurance and personally to get away sometimes. Without the changes Steve pushed on me, and without my team's support, I'd have had to take some type of leave, trading off salary to be able to care for Shane. It would have been hard to live with those regrets.

Balance is hard. It doesn't happen immediately, and it isn't static. Throughout my husband's illness and in the time after he passed away, I've had to define and redefine a new normal and forge a new balance. I continue to do my job and do it well. I still have bad days, everyone does, but I know my priorities, and no one on my team has made me feel at risk because I've had to reconfigure my balance in a very different way.

I try to be disciplined about my time. I start and end my workday early. I rarely check email after hours, and I even have lunch with my son at school occasionally. My colleagues and clients know that if they call after the bus comes, my son is here. My son knows that he's my priority, and sometimes I need to work in the evening or on the weekend, but it's not my norm. My team knows my priorities, too. They know I'm not willing to give up time with my family. I know what can happen, and that tradeoff isn't worth it. I'm grateful I work with a group that gets it.

Life looks so different now, but it would be unrecognizable if Steve hadn't taken a risk that put my welfare as a person over a temporary business objective. I wouldn't have gone to Arizona, had my son, become a stepmom to two wonderful boys, or been in a position to balance my work and family through a tragedy.

What I learned from Steve was a gift: professional and personal success aren't mutually exclusive.

Steve and I are friends now, but it took time for me to see what he was trying to do: inspire and challenge me and my colleagues to navigate our personal and professional lives to find a balance.

I'm a team manager now, and I work hard to pass along Steve's message, which is captured in this book.

Balance is different for everyone; you just have to find yours. It won't be easy, but I hope his message challenges and inspires you the way it did for me and that you pass it along to your teams and colleagues. I promise it will be worth it!

PART I

A RUDDERLESS SHIP

Not to have control over the senses is like sailing in a rudderless ship, bound to break to pieces on coming in contact with the very first rock.

~ Mahatma Gandhi

CHAPTER 1

THE CRASH

A smooth sea never made a skillful mariner.

~ English Proverb

It was a cool Sunday morning, only days before Christmas. I awoke hungover from another exhausting week of work. It was the fifth or sixth consecutive week of a *working* Saturday. But who's counting?

I had little idea what the day's schedule would be. All I knew was that my wife was always busy. There were gifts still to buy, decorations to hang, company to prepare for, charitable activities to serve, and a family of four to support. Or so it seemed. My family was always going in one direction, and I was going in the other.

Christmas had ceased to be fun. It was just another thing on an overly burdened calendar. Reality hit me that today was probably my only chance to go Christmas shopping. Of course, I could find out what "we" got for the kids on Christmas itself, but I had to at least have a gift or two for my wife.

Although I was raised to honor the Sabbath, church was an afterthought. The nurturing of my family and my soul could wait; there was work to be done. So, as I made my way downstairs, I told my wife I would be heading to the mall to do some last-minute shopping. And then, for the first time, I asked what she might like for Christmas. Instead of answering, she responded with a question that perhaps revealed what she really wanted.

"Did you get all of your work done last night?"

"Yes," I lied.

"Good. I'll need your help this afternoon cleaning the house and finishing the decorating. My parents are coming on Tuesday, and we need to be prepared. I plan to run to the store after I drop EJ off at her eleven o'clock playdate. I need to make an appetizer for the holiday potluck dinner with the neighbors. The babysitter will be here just before five o'clock . . ."

The list seemed to go on indefinitely. As was my nature, I didn't want to disappoint. "No problem," I responded, stretching the truth for a second time that morning. "I'll run to the mall and return to help with anything you need."

Sensing the tension and exhaustion in my wife (that I too was feeling), I offered to take our three-year-old son with me. "Why don't I take the little guy to the store? Perhaps you can get some rest or exercise after dropping our daughter off."

"That would be great," she responded, not having a clue as to how our world would be rocked that day.

Later that morning, I strapped my son into the car seat of our Honda Odyssey and made my way to the mall, one of my least favorite places in the world, especially when Monday work deadlines loomed.

As we entered the mall, I had a singular focus—get in and out as quickly as possible. To this day, I don't remember what I bought my wife. I do know that I visited three stores and left with three bags. On the way out, my son asked if he could see Santa. I told him the line was too long. We left the mall in record time. I had work to do.

As I drove home, I checked my email to see if my colleagues had any comments on the document I had drafted and distributed the day before. The client expected the deliverable first thing Monday morning. I read two email responses while driving with my three-year-old son in the back seat. Who does that?

The feedback from my colleagues felt like a punch in the gut. Their suggestions were good, but I was disappointed. And, it meant more work. As I drove up our steep driveway and pulled into the garage, my mind was fully consumed with how to respond to my colleagues, complete my work, and do something else my wife had requested (although by now I'd forgotten what it was).

I glanced in the rearview mirror and for the first time noticed that my son was sound asleep. I decided to leave the music on and let him rest. I rushed into the house and fired up the computer. I had already written my email response to my colleagues in my head.

After hitting "send" on my email committing to make the necessary updates later that evening, I went back to the garage and collected my shopping bags. My son was still asleep. I hid the bags inside and chatted with my wife, who was now baking in the kitchen.

After another five minutes or so, I returned to the garage to check on my son. As I opened the door and stepped into the garage, I noticed the van moving ever so slightly. Within an instant, the van picked up speed as it began backing down our steep driveway.

I screamed, "STOP!" hoping the perpetrator would instantly reconsider the theft of my car and, more importantly, my son.

I then realized there was no driver as I helplessly chased the car. Recognizing the futility of my mission, I collapsed in our front yard and watched as the van picked up speed, crossed the street, hopped the curb, and slammed into our neighbor's front porch.

As their awning collapsed on the roof of the car, I gathered myself and sprinted down the driveway and across the street, ignoring the frantic question from my wife, "What happened!?" followed promptly by "OH MY GOD!"

I pried open the side door of the van. My son sat motionless with his eyes closed. I began shaking him and saying his name. Still sleepy, he opened his eyes and said, "Hey Pappa." I hugged my son tight, thanked my God, and promised to seek a better way.

Chapter 2

The Root Cause

*Zombie [zom bee], noun—a person who is or appears
to be lifeless, apathetic, or totally lacking in independent
judgment; automaton.*

~ Collins English Dictionary

The next several hours were a blur. I carried my son to my wife and desperately tried to explain to her what had happened. "The car slipped gears . . . the emergency brake malfunctioned. . . ." (Note: The car was in neutral, and the brake was not applied.)

I painfully watched as my neighbors returned to find a Honda Odyssey parked on their front porch. I hung my head in shame as I worked with the local police to dislodge the van and send it away for repairs. (Can I go too?)

Though my wife was sympathetic, she knew the source of the problem. The problem was me. Simply put, I was not present. I was constantly preoccupied with one area of my life at the expense of all others. And just like my son was in the passenger seat of an unmanned vehicle, so too was I in the passenger seat of the vehicle called my life.

Ever since I was a child, I was eager to please. Growing up in the blue-collar town of Pittsburgh, Pennsylvania, with the Steelers dominating the NFL, I thought that any self-respecting athlete played football. My older brother was a football star, and I saw how proud my parents were. I was too. I was determined to be the next Terry Bradshaw.

So, I scrapped my way through high school with the intent to play at the highest level that I could. I followed my brother's footsteps to the

College of William and Mary. Recognizing the dream of playing quarterback was not to be, the coaches played me as an outside linebacker. I like to say that what I lacked in size, I made up for with a lack of speed. At least I would have a great education to fall back on.

By the time I graduated, I was certain of the formula for success and happiness. Get a good job, pursue the advanced degree, marry the pretty girl, earn the next promotion, buy the house on the cul-de-sac, build the bank account, have the two kids, and live happily ever after.

I methodically pursued this course of action. Yet, although I had checked all the boxes, I found myself asking: Why am I so stressed? Why am I exhausted? Why am I unfulfilled? Why am I a zombie going through the motions at work and in life?

While I lacked the self-awareness to realize it on that fateful December day, I grew to understand that I was a thin-skinned, perfectionist, eager-to-please guy with an inability to say no. I had no real purpose in my life other than the pursuit of everyone's approval. If a client challenged me or I perceived a slight from a colleague, the issue would eat away at me. As work demands and deadlines became more frequent and significant, I refused to set boundaries and failed at effective delegation.

Though I professed to my wife and kids that no one was more important, I certainly didn't convey it by my actions. My work consumed me. And although I said that faith was the dominant force in my life, that was simply another way to craft the story I sold to others. I didn't actually live that way.

By my early thirties, I was struggling to make it home for dinner with my family. And when I was home, I was rarely mentally or emotionally present. My cell phone and email were pervasive, and I lacked the discipline to shut them off. I had high blood pressure and needed medication to sleep through the night. I had no purpose or direction. I was disengaged and unfulfilled. I lacked balance and was heading for a crash—literally.

If you can relate to this story, *this book is for you.*

If you are a disengaged zombie in the workforce or in life, *this book is for you.*

If you are or aspire to be a leader in business or in life, *this book is for you.*

And, if you seek fulfillment and to make a positive impact in the world, *this book is for you.*

Chapter 3

The Better Way

*The great danger for most of us lies not in setting
our aim too high and falling short, but in setting
our aim too low and hitting the mark.*

~ Michelangelo

I profusely apologized to my wife in the immediate aftermath of the incident that has become known in my neighborhood as the inspiration behind self-driving vehicles. I accepted responsibility for the incident, but I had yet to accept responsibility for the root cause. I blamed my boss, my clients, and my colleagues for unreasonable work demands that consumed my every waking thought. I told my wife that I would prepare my resume over the holidays and pursue a more reasonable job and employer. Surely that would right the ship and set our course straight to joy and fulfillment—just like Santa Claus was certain to come down our chimney that Christmas Eve.

It was naïve thinking.

I took my dog for a walk on the dark and cold night before Christmas. For the first time in weeks, my head was clear. I heard music and laughter in the distance. I was present to the decorations on our neighbors' homes. The smell of a backyard bonfire wafted through the air. The stars were out in force. When we reached the newly constructed park at the end of the neighborhood, I took a seat on a bench. And then, there was silence.

I don't know how long I sat on that bench. I do know it was the first time I had cried in several years. I also sent to the heavens a sincere and meaningful prayer; something else I hadn't done in years. My grief and pain uncovered a clear message.

My challenges at work weren't caused by my clients or colleagues. My challenges at home were self-inflicted. *I* was the only person present in all circumstances. Until I took ownership and personal responsibility for my own balance and fulfillment, I would never have it. The grass wouldn't be greener somewhere else.

Perhaps you've seen the 1996 hit movie, *Jerry McGuire*. In that movie, Tom Cruise portrays a sports agent who discovers his conscience. He had become wrapped up in a business with disingenuous motives and questionable tactics. One night, he decides to write a new mission statement in the form of a company-wide memo that describes a better way to do business.

When the dog and I returned home from our walk, I had my own *Jerry McGuire* moment. While I don't mean to imply that my company employed questionable tactics, I did experience my own crisis of conscience. I knew there had to be a better way for me.

Rather than seek a new job, I first sought a new self. I decided to apply the same management consulting skills I leveraged at work to my life. For the first time, I developed my own personal strategic plan, my own mission statement. Between Christmas and New Year's, I drafted the following:

Mission

To have a significant positive impact on the integrity, happiness, and self-worth of children and families via avenues available or intentionally created at work, at home, and in the community.

Goals

1. *Family:* Provide an example of a life of integrity and fun within my own family.
2. *Faith:* Demonstrate faith and its value through my actions.
3. *Work:* Establish myself as a leader fostering environments of integrity and life balance.

4. *Community:* Pursue local venues to impact the lives of children and families.

5. *Stretch:* Pursue life-changing avenues to impact others on a broader scale.

Objectives

Family: Provide an example of a life of integrity and fun within my own family.

1. Remain faithful and loving to my wife.
2. Be generous with my time and patient with my children.
3. Make an ongoing priority to eat and pray with my family.
4. Leverage adversity as an opportunity to teach.
5. Pursue fun and educational vacations/forums as a family unit twice a year.
6. Respect and support my parents, siblings, and other relatives.

Faith: Demonstrate faith and its value through my actions.

1. Attend church regularly as a family unit.
2. Read and study the Bible and Christian faith.
3. Pursue one or more mission-like activities as a family unit.
4. Consider baptism as an independent adult decision.
5. Volunteer in some capacity in youth ministry.

Work: Establish self as a leader fostering environments of integrity and life balance.

1. Pursue career opportunities whereby I can leverage my role as a leader.
2. Publish, communicate, and teach a set of values-based principles.
3. Engage subject-matter experts to reinforce values.
4. Pursue family-friendly outings and celebrations.
5. Engage a leadership coach and serve in that capacity for others.

Community: Pursue local venues to impact the lives of children and families.

1. Influence and encourage children as a coach of youth sports activities.
2. Pursue speaking engagements with local schools, churches, or other organizations.
3. Identify and support one or more local charitable organizations focused on supporting the development of kids facing difficult challenges.

Stretch: Pursue life-changing avenues to impact others on a broader scale.

1. Pursue a career change driven by my personal mission—start my own business.
2. Develop a niche as a motivational speaker for business professionals, children, and/or families.
3. Write an inspirational book for business professionals lost in their career and life.

The mission I crafted was a deep reflection of my personal values and life experiences to that point. I've always been a kid at heart. I love sports. I love to teach. I love to coach. I value time with family. I believe a parent's love and influence is critical to a child's development. I honor those who work hard on behalf of others. I have great empathy for those who suffer from anxiety, stress, and depression. And, it simply breaks my heart to see a child suffer.

However, I had to wrestle with the tension of my career. How in the world do I reconcile a personal mission to positively impact the integrity, happiness, and self-worth of children and families with my current job as a business and technology consultant to the federal government? Do I give up the six-figure salary to pursue a new career as a teacher or coach? Do I drop everything and find the *right* nonprofit to serve? How do I sustain our current lifestyle, pay the bills, and position my children for a bright and successful future?

I put those concerns aside for the time being and started with my life outside of work. If my current employment and career is a necessary constraint, what else could I do in pursuit of my mission and life goals? I took a counterintuitive approach for someone struggling with balance. Instead of taking things off my plate, I identified and pursued activities that aligned with my values and purpose:

- I committed to nightly dinner with the family.
- I volunteered as a coach of youth basketball and baseball.
- I established weekly lunch dates with my wife.
- I volunteered monthly as a youth minister.
- I committed to an annual vacation at a YMCA family camp.
- I joined the Y-Princess/Y-Guides programs for focused time with my daughter and son.
- I initiated an annual fund-raiser to adopt the wish of a child facing a life-threatening illness.
- I committed to daily exercise and weekly basketball with friends.

I made these and other commitments, knowing full well that there would be consequences in my job and career. I put nonnegotiable boundaries on my availability for work. For the first time in my life, I intentionally articulated and restored my life priorities. I apprehensively convinced myself that I was willing to accept the consequences of my new commitments.

Eventually, I shared my personal strategic plan and these commitments with my wife. Though supportive, she was understandably skeptical. How could someone so clearly overwhelmed and consumed by a demanding job find the time to pursue such lofty aspirations? "I'll be happy if you just showed up at home," she said.

I accepted the critique without judgment. I had to earn her trust, as well as my own.

Just to be clear, I worked very hard *before* embarking on this new plan, and I *continued* to work very hard after. The simple act of stating my priorities in life and making commitments consistent with those priorities forced healthy habits that filled my tank. More to come on this later.

I returned to work with a new purpose in the new year. On my first day back in the office, I took my plan one step further. I reviewed my job description.

At the time, I was a project manager and technical director at SRA International. My job was to plan, execute, monitor, and control projects to deliver in accordance with contract and client expectations. I was also responsible for supporting other project teams and ensuring the quality of products and services delivered across a portfolio of contracts serving our environmental account. I had added responsibilities to contribute to the growth of our business and the management of our staff.

I sat at my desk that early January morning reading my formal job description. It was nearly two pages in length and included a dozen bullet points of mundane requirements. For years, I had always struggled to answer the question posed by friends and family: "What do you do?" Usually, my vague response served as a quick transition to a conversation about sports or the weather. If I was not inspired by my job, why would anyone else be interested?

I decided it was time to rewrite my job description. I fired up the computer and pulled up my personal strategic plan. I spent a half hour writing and editing various statements that attempted to connect my personal mission to my job. Eventually, I settled on a one-sentence job description:

> *I inspire and empower my colleagues to be successful*
> *in their personal and professional lives.*

That was it. Surely, I was not the only one on my team of ten, within an account of about one hundred, and a company of approximately seven thousand, who struggled with balance. There must be others struggling to be the best husband, wife, father, mother, brother, sister, or friend they could be while delivering excellence on behalf of the company and its clients.

Through the simple act of rewriting my job description, I revised my job to be consistent with my mission and values. While I still adhered to the requirements of my job, I fundamentally changed the way I went about my work. To be clear, this did not happen overnight. It took intentional effort sustained over an extended period. I blocked off time on my calendar to pursue strategic activities that directly supported my revised job description. I sometimes had to forgo the perpetually urgent to support the important. Admittedly, I missed some commitments initially. Eventually, I learned to manage my commitments better.

Ultimately, I transitioned from a pacesetter leadership style to an authoritative leader and coach. I no longer assumed individual responsibility for the delivery of quality products and services within unreasonable time constraints. I engaged teams and practiced delegation. With considerable help from my wife and a leadership coach, I began to recognize the negative impacts of my constant search for affirmation. I took greater risks and brought my authentic self to work, accepting that I could not please everyone.

Within one year, I was asked to lead our environmental account with full profit/loss responsibility for a broad portfolio of contracts. I leveraged this opportunity to further the impact of my new mission. I understood and embraced the self-imposed challenge to transition from a manager to a leader.

I defined and preached a set of values and principles that would guide our account, not the least of which was balance. I reinforced those values in creative and intentional ways. I facilitated quarterly All-Hands meetings, focusing less on what we did and more on how we did it. In a world of commoditized products and services, we decided that our values served as our primary discriminator in the marketplace as well as in our individual lives.

I even embraced my passion for children and families as a leader of our account. I organized a book drive for inner-city children in combination with our client's annual summit in Philadelphia. While our contracting peers were throwing evening parties for their clients, we were engaging our clients by helping to equip needy children with books that would educate the next generation of environmental stewards. Our clients loved it, and the book drives continued for several years.

We planned family-friendly outings. We celebrated marriages and births. We added personal life goals as part of professional development plans and objectives. We engaged guest speakers promoting mental, physical, and spiritual health. We embraced vacations without computers or phones. We set the example for providing honest feedback in an empathetic manner. All along, I demonstrated what it meant to be an authentic leader by openly sharing my personal struggles, insecurities, and dreams.

What began with great apprehension and uncertainty turned into the best and most rewarding years of my career. At my lowest point, I was a disengaged zombie in the workforce. I was a victim, convinced that the grass would be greener somewhere else. Instead, I pursued a personal mission and brought my authentic self to work. Seven years after embarking on a personal journey to restore my priorities and redefine my job description, I went from managing a team of ten people and $2 million of annual business to leading an account of approximately four hundred people and $80 million of annual business. The account I led far exceeded average engagement scores across the company, and our staff turnover was among the lowest every year.

I was promoted in job or title three times and increased my compensation by nearly 70 percent. Most importantly, I received the Chairman's Award for Honesty and Service that's given to the one individual in the company of seven thousand employees who best exemplifies the ethics of service to clients, colleagues, and the community.

While the numbers and recognition are noteworthy, they were not the point. The objective was never about money or the growth and profitability targets provided by my superiors. I didn't seek to hit the lottery or climb the corporate ladder. Any such measures or so-called accomplishments were simply the results of serving our clients and our colleagues.

The point was the successful fulfillment of the new job description I had written. I sought to inspire and empower my colleagues to be successful in their personal and professional lives, just as I sought to do the same for myself.

The greatest satisfaction I take away from my experience at SRA is the impact I had on the professional and personal development of my colleagues. In March 2013, I chose to leave SRA on my own terms and at peace with a job well done. I wasn't running away from a problem. I was no longer a victim blaming others. Rather, I was an inspired human being seeking to check another goal off the personal strategic plan I had written seven years earlier—pursue a career change driven by my personal mission.

Thus, I founded CEEK LLC (pronounced "Seek") with the original mission to inspire and empower individuals and organizations to succeed. The foundation of CEEK is the "7C's Model." Our name is not an acronym. Rather, it represents intentional effort to "seek" balance and fulfillment in our work and our lives. Our tagline, *CEEK a Better Way*, serves as a motivating force behind everything we do as individuals and as an organization.

In response to my resignation from SRA, I received dozens of phone calls and well over a hundred email messages from many of my colleagues. A few are below. These represent the general themes of most of the messages I received:

- "You have always given me the respect, flexibility, and support to stretch myself, pursue my goals, and make my own mistakes. I want to thank you for the inspiration and soul that you have given to me and to this Account."
- "You are one of the most honest, ethical, truly caring, and professional people I know, and you instilled that in how you ran your account and the people that you led."

- "You have truly shown me what it means to be a leader, not just a 'manager,' and to understand that feeding my soul will come back in spades to feed my career."

- "You have been my breath of fresh air, and I embrace your outlook on life. Like you, I strive each day to make a positive difference in this world. You are special, and I feel blessed to have met you."

- "From our first phone conversation, your efforts to promote balance between the competing needs of family and work and doing what is right for your clients, not just what is profitable, was made clear to me. In my experience, this is a rare and treasured character in the business world."

- "You have always been my reminder about work balance, and if you had not made the changes you made a few years ago, I am certain I would not have gotten married and would not have my son, who is a true blessing and my greatest gift." (Sent to me from the author of the foreword of this book.)

I can't help but wonder what would have become of me and my colleagues had I chosen a different path seven years ago. I certainly would not have been an inspiration to hundreds of my colleagues or made the impact I did. It was real. It was tangible and life-changing—for the better. I came to realize that I could bring a unique and authentic mission to my job regardless of industry, location, or position.

 An Important Side Note

> For those of us struggling with a purpose in life, look no further than the people you interact with every day. Your life matters. Your interactions matter.

Had I not set a new course for my life, I'm quite certain that I would have bounced from job to job as another disengaged zombie in the workforce. And at home, perhaps I would have remained a caring husband

and father in words but not action, incapable of true presence, constantly striving for unattainable affirmation, unhealthy, and unfulfilled.

Instead, I chose a better way. I took the CONN, a common term referring to the act of taking control of a ship's movement. I set a new course for my life. As a result, I am inspired. I am fulfilled. I have healthy relationships with my wife, my children, and my creator. My latest blood pressure reading was 120 over 78, and I no longer need prescription medication to sleep through the night. And though I deal with many of the same life struggles as everyone else, I am at peace.

My pursuit of healthy balance has been and remains the key to my engagement at work, my fulfillment at home, and my peace of mind, body, and spirit. Throughout my journey, I have discovered some basic realities and myths regarding healthy life balance. I share those with you now.

CHAPTER 4

THE DISCOVERY

*Ignorance (I don't know) is not the opposite
of learning—it's the threshold of learning.*

~ Chalmers Brothers

You may have already noticed that I don't use the term Work/Life Balance in this book. While most of us are familiar with that term, I believe it reflects a problem in and of itself. We seem to view work and life as two separate entities.

Last I checked, work is a part of my life. So too are my family, my faith, my health, my hobbies, etc. By thinking of Work and Life as separate elements of a Balance equation, we're pursuing a goal that symbolically equates work and life.

Worse yet, we often associate our personal value with our job or career. We define ourselves by what we do as opposed to who we are. Our culture reinforces this notion. How often does someone inquire about the person you are? How do you respond when someone asks, "What do you do?" (More to come on this in PART II.)

With all due respect to every profession, even those that save lives, your work is not as precious as your life. Perhaps you've heard stories about individuals who literally work themselves into severe illness and even death. Many of you reading this now know that the priority you have placed on your work and career has come at the expense of aspects of life that you profess to be of greater priority.

BREAKING NEWS: Someone else will perform your job at some point in the future. It's not unique to you. No one else can replace your role as a father, mother, son, daughter, brother, sister, friend, colleague, etc. These roles are unique to you. As renowned author and spiritual leader Andy Stanley says, "Never sacrifice what's unique to you, for something someone else will do."

Don't get me wrong; I understand your work and career are important. In some cases, we must focus our time and attention on work as a top priority in our lives. As an extreme example, Nelson Mandela sacrificed the relationships with his family in favor of a greater cause. While not desired or preferred, the sacrifices he made were worthwhile. As he acknowledged in his autobiography, *Long Walk to Freedom*, Mandela did not choose to place the people of South Africa ahead of his family. However, he discovered that his calling and life's work prevented him from being the husband, father, son, and brother that he wanted to be. He sacrificed those he knew best and loved most for the benefit of millions he would never know.

Fortunately, most of us will not have to spend twenty-seven years in prison to serve a higher purpose, and it's easy to find examples where many of us are asked to make sacrifices to our families and life balance due to important demands of our profession.

- Last year, I watched the director of the Federal Emergency Management Agency (FEMA) on television responding to questions in the aftermath of Hurricanes Harvey, Irma, and Maria that crushed Texas, Florida, and Puerto Rico, respectively. I'm quite certain that the Director and his staff had not slept well or seen their families for several weeks.
- Those in our military often sacrifice personal priorities and life balance for a far greater cause. Their personal pursuit of balance may be suspended for our benefit for several months and even years in service to their fellow man.
- Our first responders and medical professionals are often engaged without notice to serve others and save lives. Their call to serve will often come at the expense of other personal priorities and life demands.

You don't have to be responding to emergencies or in the business of protecting and saving lives to experience similar tensions in your pursuit of healthy balance. Perhaps you're a single parent holding two jobs just to make ends meet. Or, maybe you're a student or an aspiring entrepreneur investing considerable time and effort to build a better life for yourself and those closest to you. Or, maybe you're the primary bread-winner in the household who feels the pressure to sustain your job or to advance in your career to serve the current and future needs of your family.

Whatever your profession and life circumstances, sometimes work may require intense periods of focus at the expense of other priorities. In many cases, those periods are dictated by events outside of our direct control (e.g., three hurricanes in three weeks, a nine-month deployment, or a critical project deadline). Similarly, life can throw significant challenges your way. Perhaps you recently endured an illness, lost a loved one, or experienced a failed relationship.

Such circumstances will always place a strain on your life balance equation. The important thing to remember is that life balance is a tension to be managed, not a problem to be solved. There is no "ta-dah" moment where you exclaim, "I finally discovered healthy balance!" If you have healthy balance now, you will be tested later. If you lack healthy balance now, you can employ the tools and ideas in this book to help discover and sustain it. Regardless, the tension will always be there. The question isn't what you can do to discover healthy balance, but rather what you can do to manage the tension effectively.

This book offers a formula for the pursuit of healthy life balance in a manner that will manage this tension well. By proactively and intentionally managing this tension, you can achieve healthy balance and be better equipped to handle brief or extended periods of disruption and adversity.

In my personal pursuit of balance, I've learned many valuable lessons that are conveyed throughout this book. The most significant lessons regarding balance I've learned are below in the form of three prominent realities and three prominent myths.

Realities

We can observe and learn many of the realities of life balance from the world of sports and fitness—where physical balance is critical to success. Simply stated, these realities include:

1. If you lack balance, you will fall.
2. Sprinters never last.
3. Overuse leads to injury.

First, if you lack balance, you will fall. Just like a gymnast may fall from the balance beam if she loses her balance, you too (or those closest to you) will fall without proper life balance. While the result may not be as sudden, the impact can be far greater: years of regret, failed relationships, illness and disease, the list goes on.

In my early thirties, my work was pervasive. I told my wife and children that no one was more important, but I didn't demonstrate it through my actions. While I believed that faith was foundational to my core being, it took a backseat to the demands of my job. And while I valued fitness and health as a former athlete, I didn't commit the time to sustain it.

Simply put, my professed priorities were inconsistent with my demonstrated behaviors. Work defined me and consumed all aspects of my physical and mental being. I lacked balance, and as a result, my relationships with my wife and children were fragmented. My spiritual foundation was lacking. And, I was physically unhealthy. Ultimately, my lack of balance was the root cause of the incident that sent my son crashing into the neighbor's porch. I had fallen.

> In what aspects of your life are professed priorities inconsistent with your demonstrated behaviors?
>
> What warning signs exist that you're falling or headed for a fall?

Second, sprinters never last. Even the most elite athletes in the world can't sustain a sprinter's pace indefinitely. They must eventually pause; they must rest; they must refuel.

In his book *The Monk Who Sold His Ferrari*, Robin Sharma likens our lives to that of a high-performing machine. If you purchased a high-performing vehicle, would you run the vehicle nonstop without a periodic pause to cool the engine, refuel, and change the oil?

I took off in my career at a dead sprint. I was eager to please and determined to succeed. This seemed sustainable as a bachelor in my twenties but persisted as a bad habit that lacked strategic focus and clarity of personal values and life priorities. Eventually, I fell in love, got married, and had two kids and a dog. As competing demands grew exponentially, it became apparent that I hadn't learned the discipline necessary to pause or the importance of filling my tank.

Stephen Covey wisely defined the seventh (and most important) habit of highly effective people as "Sharpen the Saw." This is a metaphor for the simple act to preserve, refresh, and enhance your physical, spiritual, mental, and social/emotional well-being. And, just like pausing to sharpen the saw can greatly enhance the productivity of the lumberjack, so too can pausing to sharpen your physical, spiritual, mental, and social/emotional well-being enhance your productivity and fulfillment.

> In what aspects of your life do you need to refuel or "sharpen the saw?"
> What warning signs exist that you're running out of gas?

Third, overuse leads to injury. In a study published in the May 2017 issue of the *American Journal of Sports Medicine*, University of Wisconsin researchers found that young athletes who participate in their primary sport for more than eight months in a year were more likely to report overuse injuries. This seems to be a statement of the obvious. Perhaps more concerning are reports from the American Academy of Pediatrics that discovered a higher prevalence of burnout, anxiety, depression, and attrition among children who specialize early in a single activity. Just like the specialization of young athletes leads to a higher incidence of physical and mental injury, so too will a specialization or singular focus on work to the neglect of other personal priorities lead to physical or mental injury.

My job was the priority focus of my life for years. Work defined and consumed me. Even when I participated in activities associated with family, faith, or friends, work always crept into my thoughts. I was always preoccupied and rarely paid full attention to these and other important aspects of my life. I wasn't able to experience joy. I was checked out.

My singular job focus taxed my physical and mental well-being. I developed high blood pressure in my early thirties. And, even though I was physically and mentally exhausted, I experienced many sleepless nights. I didn't know who I was or what I even desired in life. Not surprisingly, I ruptured my Achilles tendon during a rare night of basketball with friends. I was uninspired. I was depressed. I was injured.

> In what areas of your life does overuse come at the expense of other priorities?
>
> What warning signs can you see of impending mental, physical, or spiritual injury?

Myths

Many of us attribute a lack of life balance to current circumstances. Perhaps, as I did, you blame the boss, the client, or your colleagues. We tell ourselves it'll get better when circumstances change. It won't. Until you accept personal responsibility for your balance, you'll never have it. Below are three commonly held myths about life balance that we'll explore to expose the false assumptions they're based on:

1. Balance is attained by working less and playing more.

2. Life will be easy once I find the proper balance.

3. Personal and professional success are mutually exclusive.

First, balance is attained by working less and playing more. As an executive coach, I'm often asked how I define balance. That's the wrong question. Balance is not universally defined. It means different things to different people and changes depending on the circumstances of your life. The better question is this: How do you define balance?

My clients often answer this question with a general statement about spending less time at work and more time with family and friends. Defining balance in such terms isn't attainable. While working less or playing more may help in some cases, there's always the potential for more or less. In other words, how can you determine when you have sufficiently attained more or less?

It's important to understand that balance is not a "thing." Balance isn't black or white. Our sense of balance is a personal assessment that is neither true or false. As Chalmers Brothers astutely explains in his book, *Language and the Pursuit of Happiness*, "We often treat our assessments as though they are assertions—as though they are facts." And in this case, we treat our assessment of balance as though we have it or we don't, without even defining what *it* is.

In order to effectively manage the tension of balance, it's necessary to explore the standards you believe define healthy balance. Until the incident with my son, I never took the time to assess my personal mission, values, and priorities. After doing so, I was better able to define balance based on my current circumstances and priorities. Only then could I begin to make tangible (and measurable) progress toward healthy balance. As you will soon learn, balance is best defined and most readily achieved when your demonstrated behaviors are consistent with your professed priorities.

How do you define healthy life balance?

Second, life will be easy once I find the proper balance. Finding sustainable balance doesn't mean that life won't throw significant challenges your way. Sometimes bad things happen to good people. However, the preventive maintenance associated with balance can sustain and improve your health and relationships. And when life throws you a curveball, you'll be better equipped to handle it.

One of my spiritual mentors, Steve Daugherty, the author of *Experiments in Honesty: Meditations on Love, Fear and the Honest to God Naked Truth* and a pastor at Crosspointe Church, in Cary, North Carolina, helped me understand that healthy balance promotes *pre-crisis integrity*. In other words, if you apply the discipline necessary to sustain healthy balance, you'll be better equipped to handle adversity when it inevitably arises. This may be in the form of a looming deadline or crisis at work that requires focused attention for a brief or extended period. Alternatively, this may be adversity at home, illness, loss of a loved one, a child suffering, a financial setback, a broken relationship, or some other unexpected event.

Whatever the case, healthy balance doesn't mean you or those closest to you won't experience difficult times; we all do. Healthy balance equips you with the strength and perspective to persevere and overcome. Without healthy balance or pre-crisis integrity, the next incident or adversity you face may be the one that pushes you over the edge where you fall, run out of gas, or sustain irrevocable injury.

> Are you mentally, physically, and spiritually prepared for the *next* unanticipated event or adversity?

Third, personal and professional success are mutually exclusive. While balance may not be necessary for professional success, it certainly isn't counter to it. A simple Google search reveals numerous studies and analyses demonstrating the positive impact of healthy life balance practices in organizations. The most common benefits include enhanced productivity, improved morale, reduced absenteeism, and lower turnover. Organizations that promote and support healthy balance policies report higher engagement and trust, which correlate directly to enhanced business results.

Such concepts aren't new. Steven Covey recognized the significance of balance in *The 7 Habits of Highly Effective People* where he conveys that balance is the key to effectiveness. Dr. Covey was referring to the balance between productivity and production capability, or what he referred to as P and PC. If you don't pause to "Sharpen the Saw," you'll diminish your productivity.

Effective life balance will enhance, not hinder, your productivity at work and at home. It's the key to sustainable personal and professional success. In my experience, balance was necessary for professional success. Once I learned to manage the tension well, I became more engaged at work and experienced the best years of my professional career. I also became more fulfilled in life and can honestly say that I have no regrets relative to the father, husband, and person that I have grown to be.

As conveyed in the second myth, my life isn't easy, nor do I expect it to be. I still work very hard, and my family faces challenges just like anyone else. However, I remain intentional in my efforts to restore my mind, body, and spirit. As a result, I'm more focused, present, and productive at work and at home.

> How might the effective pursuit of life balance enhance
> your productivity and professional success?

If you struggle to answer any of the questions associated with the myths presented in this section, don't worry. You're not alone. PART II of this book will take you on a journey of self-discovery and awareness. We'll revisit many of the realities and myths of life balance as we *CEEK a Better Way* to navigate chaos in pursuit of PEACE.

PART II

THE PATH TO PEACE

*How could a person possibly lead a corporation if he
cannot even lead himself? How could you nurture a family
if you haven't learned to nurture and care for yourself?
How could you possibly do good if you don't even feel
good?*

~ Robin Sharma

In his book *The Monk Who Sold His Ferrari*, Robin Sharma tells the
story of a lawyer who neglected his health, his relationships, and other
life priorities in pursuit of a successful legal career. After suffering
a heart attack, the lawyer travels to the Himalayas for a life-altering
experience with a monk named Yogi. I believe the lesson of this
instructive tale is best summed up in the following story from the
book.

> One night a father was relaxing with his newspaper after a
> long day at the office. His son, who wanted to play, kept on
> pestering him. Finally, fed up, the father ripped out a picture
> of the globe that was in the paper and tore it into a hundred

tiny pieces. "Here, son, go ahead and try to put this back together," he said, hoping that this would keep the little boy busy long enough for him to finish reading his paper. To his amazement, his son returned after only one minute with the globe perfectly back together. When the startled father asked how he achieved this feat, the son smiled gently and replied, "Dad, on the other side of the globe there was a picture of a person, and once I got the person together, the world was okay." (Robin Sharma, *The Monk Who Sold His Ferrari: A Remarkable Story About Living Your Dreams* [New York: HarperCollins Publishers, 2011], 201)

It's easy for us to become consumed by the demands of a job, the family, or other life priorities. We have so much to do—too much to do. We keep our heads down and press on with whatever seems to be the most urgent priority of the moment: the email; the meeting; the looming deadline; the carpool; the housework; or that discussion with my significant other that I put off for another day, week, or even a year.

The chaos distracts us. The urgency consumes us. We convince ourselves things will settle down when circumstances change. When I get that promotion, I'll have more control. When we hit that project milestone, the pace will lessen. When the kids are out of diapers, we'll have more flexibility. And when they're off to college or out of the house, we can finally relax.

We live our lives hour by hour, day by day without intentional design. We lose touch with who we were or who we thought we wanted to be. Maybe you're sitting in the passenger seat of the vehicle you call your life. Imagine what life might be like if you switched seats. Envision a new "you" as you assume control of your vessel, your life.

Today is the beginning of the new you with a new mission. Today is the day you embark on a journey to restore your priorities, presence, positive disposition, and wholeness. Today is the day you will look back on as the triggering event in your pursuit of healthy balance, fulfillment, and PEACE.

PART II of this book offers a strategy for you to take back control of your life in pursuit of healthy balance. Of the eleven chapters included in PART II, five are dedicated to the primary steps necessary to discover healthy balance:

- Pursue *A* Mission (Chapter 5)
- Establish Routines (Chapter 7)
- Appreciate the Moment (Chapter 9)
- Choose Your Disposition (Chapter 11)
- Embrace a Broader Integrity (Chapter 13)

Within each of these chapters, I include three subsections, for a total of fifteen subsections. At the end of each subsection, I offer three thought-provoking questions and a deeper-dive exercise for those interested in digging deeper.

If you haven't done so yet, I encourage you to start a journal to capture your thoughts to the questions posed. If desired, you can visit www.ceekllc.com/balance to download a free online journal with all of the activities and questions posed throughout the book. The simple act of putting your thoughts on paper (or computer) will significantly enhance the value attained from this book. Consider forming a small study group to collaborate with as you collectively work through the book. Discussing the book with peers will give everyone a richer experience.

If, like me, you prefer to read a book in its entirety before responding to questions or completing proposed activities, DON'T WORRY. At the end of this book, I've included a summary of all the questions and the deeper dive exercises. I also provide some guidance for study groups in a brief section called "Share the Adventure."

It's time to roll up your sleeves and dig in as you embark on a journey to navigate chaos in pursuit of healthy life balance!

CHAPTER 5

PURSUE *A* MISSION

What's more important than choosing the right thing
is choosing something.

~ Patrick Lencioni

While most of us are pretty clear on the mission of the organization we may support, can you say the same about your life? It's difficult to find balance and fulfillment in life if you haven't determined a reason for being or a driving purpose.

Ever since I was a child, I was told that God has a unique and special purpose for me. All I had to do was listen for my true calling. While I believe in the power of prayer and the impact of faith, the pressure to find my "true calling" was a little overwhelming.

I encourage you to give yourself the freedom to experiment. Select *A* mission—just one. Try it on. See how it fits. Just like your definition of balance will change over time, so too may your mission or purpose. Stop pressuring yourself to find *your* mission. As Patrick Lencioni advises in *The Three Big Questions for a Frantic Family*, choose something!

This chapter provides some guidance and examples that will help you:

1. State your values and purpose
2. Define balance in light of your priorities
3. Connect your purpose to your work

As you will soon discover, balance is more readily achieved when you connect with a purpose at work and in life.

State your values and purpose

When I speak to individuals and organizations about life balance, the most common question I'm asked is, "How do you define balance?" Before answering that question, I first challenge my clients with a question of my own: "What is your mission or purpose?" The definition of life balance is unique to each one of us. In order to define it, you must first articulate what's important to you. Until you do that, you'll continue to search for an unattainable objective.

As is the case with every successful organization, what's important to you begins with a compelling purpose or mission. An organization's mission statement serves as a guiding star to prioritize the activities of the organization. Why should you be any different? If you seek to prioritize your life's work, it begins with a well-defined mission. Define a purpose and state priorities in light of that purpose. Start with your core values. What do you care about? What do you love to do? Who do you do it for? What are your goals? How would you like to be remembered? Focus on what is meaningful to you, and then write it down.

If you're like me, or any organization that has ever drafted a mission statement and set of core values, these aren't easy questions to answer. It takes time. It takes reflection. It may be uncomfortable.

As shared in PART I of this book, I took the time to assess my values and purpose after I "crashed." I had lived my life to that point without intentional design. I was in the passenger seat of the vehicle I called my life.

My path wasn't bad, but it wasn't genuine. I had never honestly reflected on who I was as a person and the person I wanted to be. I never had, to that point, articulated my core values or a fundamental driving purpose.

While the incident with my son in the van led to a much-needed wake-up call, I certainly would have preferred to have heeded the warning signs. If only I'd taken the time to reflect earlier, would the outcome have been different? While I can't say for sure, I can only compare my general state of fulfillment, presence, peace, and balance before and after the incident, or before and after I intentionally defined balance in light of my purpose and priorities. To that, I can say the impact was significant and transformative.

Unfortunately for most of us, our tendency to assess our core values and compelling purpose only happens as a reactive response to a life-changing incident. We often hear the stories of how illness, tragedy, a damaged relationship, or other adversity changed someone's life for the better. However, such results are the exception rather than the rule. The reality is that you may not get a second chance.

If you want to be the best version of yourself, why wait? If you desire healthy balance, act now. Don't stand by on the sidelines waiting for life circumstances that force you to wrestle with questions such as "What's most important to me?" or "Why do I do what I do?" Be proactive. Create your future.

So where should you start? How can you write an effective mission statement that defines your compelling purpose and serves as a guide for your life priorities and ultimately healthy balance? Perhaps the best place to start is to look at a few examples from some of the world's most successful organizations:

- Google's mission is "to organize the world's information and make it universally accessible and useful." This statement drives the priorities and decisions on the products and services offered by Google. It is the reason they're the leading search engine and trusted source for content delivery on the web.
- Whole Foods' purpose is "to nourish people and the planet." Coupled with their core values, this mission drives their emphasis on sustainability and healthy food, as well as how they serve their clients, employees, and communities.
- The American Red Cross's mission is to "prevent and alleviate human suffering in the face of emergencies by mobilizing

the power of volunteers and the generosity of donors." Through this mission, the American Red Cross turns compassion into action. It drives their priority initiatives such as blood drives and training programs for CPR, first aid, and other life-saving techniques.

Just as individuals may face adversity that prompts an assessment or reassessment of their life's work, so too can organizations. I couldn't help but notice that Facebook recently redefined its mission to "Give people the power to build community and bring the world closer together." As it discovered its platform was being misused and perhaps in response to the negative publicity surrounding the 2016 U.S. presidential election, Facebook intentionally shifted focus in a way that alienates intolerant users, decreases the number of ads people see, and protects personal information.

Facebook recognized that its original mission statement, "making the world more open and connected," didn't communicate a positive outcome or a purpose driven by core values. It's now choosing positive impact at the potential risk of corporate revenues, thereby leveraging a revised mission in pursuit of the greater good. While I commend such positive changes, I'm sure Facebook wishes it had considered such changes sooner rather than as a perceived reaction to negative publicity. Nonetheless, I'm confident that such a change is good for its long-term prospects. Any organization that's driven by a compelling mission grounded in good, authentic values will increase its odds of success.

Through the examples of these and other organizations, we see how businesses leverage values-based mission statements to serve as a filter for determining priorities and making decisions in the face of constrained resources: time and money. Show me an organization without a clear and compelling mission statement, and I will show you a failing organization. The same can be said for individuals. Writing a mission statement can be the most important activity an individual can take toward leading a fulfilled and balanced life. It forms the basis for life-changing decisions in the midst of circumstances and emotions that affect our lives.

Years ago, I took the time to write my own personal mission statement. I started by reflecting on who I am and what I care about. I defined a set of personal core values to include Heart, Humor, Humility, and Integrity, among others.

While there are plenty of online tools to help identify or define core values, you might also consider a simple exercise that I use in my workshops. I first ask participants to identify someone they admire, and then I ask them why.

Often, our description of those we admire says much about what we value. In my case, I once answered this question by naming the late North Carolina State basketball coach and ESPN commentator Jim Valvano as that person. In addition to famously leading his underdog Wolfpack to a 1983 National Championship, Valvano is most famous for his speech delivered in 1993 after receiving the Arthur Ashe Courage and Humanitarian Award at ESPN's inaugural ESPYs award show. In his speech, he challenged all of us to laugh, to think, and to have our emotions moved to tears every day.

As I reflect on three of my most prominent core values, heart, humor, and humility, they were all revealed in the character of Jim Valvano that night at the ESPYs. Even as cancerous tumors ravaged his body, he mustered the strength to deliver an impassioned speech that remains unrivaled in the over twenty-five-year history of the ESPYs. His self-deprecating humor conveyed a relatable humility that we admire to this day. Simply put, Jim Valvano represented the heart, humor, and humility that I admire and aspire to.

Whom do you admire? Why?

Based on my reflection of Jim Valvano and other great leaders, I was able to clearly express who I am and what I care about. I value the *heart*, offering empathy, compassion, and support for others in need. I'm passionate and competitive, but I value *humility* regardless of my standing. And I value *humor* as a way to brighten the day for myself and others and to further maintain humility. I love sports and outdoor activities, using both to engage with friends, family, and children to have fun, maintain healthy habits, and teach valuable life lessons. And, I maintain the highest standards of *integrity* and believe that a sustained work ethic trumps any shortcut to temporary success and fulfillment.

To help further translate this definition of who I am and what I care about into a compelling purpose, I also wrestled with the following question: "What breaks my heart?" Years ago, I heard this question posed on a leadership podcast hosted by Andy Stanley, an inspirational speaker, author, and pastor. He challenged listeners to ask this question while pursuing a compelling life purpose.

While there are many things that break my heart, I quickly discovered that I care deeply about children. Simply put, it breaks my heart to see children suffer. I believe that a strong family foundation is critical to the mental, physical, and spiritual well-being of any child. I'm incredibly grateful for the general health of my own children. I'm moved to tears by the stories of children who suffer from life-threatening diseases or those who are simply neglected.

What breaks your heart?

I wrote a mission statement as my primary motivation for what I do, how I do it, and why after the intentional reflection of my values and asking myself many questions. For several years, this was my mission:

> *To have a significant positive impact on the integrity, happiness, and self-worth of children and families via avenues available or intentionally created at work, at home and in the community.*

I refer to this mission statement in the past tense because, when I developed it, I removed the pressure to discover a single life purpose. I acknowledge and accept that my mission may change as my life experiences evolve. I'm always open to such change and revisit my mission annually to ensure it continues to serve as a driving, compelling description of who I am, what I do, and why.

Over the years, I've made some modifications to my original mission statement. More recently, I leveraged an approach advocated by Adam Leipzig in a 2013 TEDx talk. Adam, the CEO of Entertainment Media Partners, challenged his audience to answer the following questions:

- Who are you?
- What do you love to do?
- Who do you do it for?
- What do those you do it for want or need?
- What do those you do it for get from it?

As I reflected on those questions, I noted the following as my responses to each:

- I am a husband, father, mentor, and coach.
- I love to inspire others through what I say, write, and do.
- I do this for zombies in life and for neglected children.
- These individuals seek a compelling purpose, a driving motivation, and encouragement.
- These individuals want this in order to discover peace and fulfillment in life.

I then consolidated these responses into a single revised statement of my mission:

> *I am a coach who, through words and actions, inspires zombies in life to seek a better way in pursuit of personal fulfillment and success.*

If it's not abundantly obvious, this revised mission, albeit similar to the original, was a driving force behind my motivation to write this book. It serves as a filter for the activities that I choose to support. It's a daily reminder of my reason for being and the impact I seek to have in the world.

While I've shared with you a couple of examples of how I crafted my personal mission statements, there's no single correct or best approach. Plenty of online tools are available to support your efforts to develop a compelling purpose that serves as a driving force in your pursuit of personal fulfillment and, ultimately, healthier life balance. A simple Google search on "how to draft a personal mission statement" currently reveals more than twenty-seven million options!

It's important to remember: you don't have to be famous to have a compelling purpose; you don't have to have an exotic or inspirational job to have a compelling purpose; and you don't have to seek permission or approval to have a compelling purpose. You simply have to uncover the most authentic version of yourself and determine the impact you desire to have in this world.

Consider the questions posed in this chapter. Journal your responses. Draft a mission and try it on for size as you proceed throughout the remainder of this book and your life. If you find that it doesn't fit or it wears off over time, try something new. The key is to be intentional about your purpose and priorities at this moment of your life. In doing so, you'll find that it's easier to discover fulfillment and peace as you effectively manage the tension of life balance.

 Journal – Questions to Consider

- Whom do I admire most?
- What breaks my heart?
- What do these responses reveal about my core values and my driving purpose?

 Exercise – Consider a Deeper Dive

In your journal, respond to the questions to consider and note the words, concepts, or ideas that resonate most as core values that you hold. Identify three to five values that best describe you and what you care about most deeply. Draft a personal mission statement that inspires you in a manner consistent with these values and what you care about. Write it down. Share it with others. Commit to reassess and revise this statement as necessary. Refer to this statement and your core values as you complete the other activities suggested throughout this book.

Define balance in light of your priorities

Healthy balance means different things to different people. Likewise, your perspective on balance and objectives related to it will change depending on the circumstances of your life. As someone who struggled with balance early in my career, and now as a leadership and life coach, I encourage you to define what balance means to you now and at regular intervals of your life. Write it down. Be realistic. Focus on objectives broader than working more or less.

A simple online search will expose endless attempts to define balance (or work/life balance) in a manner that can be applied generally. Most of these definitions emphasize a balance between work and other life priorities or, more broadly, achievement and enjoyment.

While perhaps helpful, such definitions are nebulous at best. As noted earlier in this book, these definitions imply that work is somehow separate and distinct from life, and/or equivalent to it. Furthermore, they offer no measurable way to assess progress toward actual balance. Rather, it's something we're intuitively supposed to know or feel:

- I sense a lack of balance when I cannot follow through on commitments to my family and/or self.
- I feel unbalanced when I consistently work nights and weekends to meet a project deadline.
- I perceive a lack of balance when I am uninspired, bored, or simply complacent in life.

Merriam-Webster defines balance as "the state of having your weight spread equally so that you do not fall." It offers a second definition as "a state in which different things occur in equal or proper amounts or have a proper amount of importance." Is your weight spread equally? Have you attributed proper value or importance to your work? To your family? To your faith? To your life?

For our purpose, this latter definition of balance is more helpful. At CEEK, we define *healthy life balance* as "a state where professed priorities are consistent with demonstrated behaviors." In contrast, we define *unhealthy life balance* as a "state where professed priorities are inconsistent with demonstrated behaviors."

This construct gives you the opportunity to clarify your personal definition of life balance by simply assessing the priorities in your life. The exercise in the previous chapter serves as the foundation for determining your priorities. Based on your mission and current circumstances, what are the priorities in your life?

I reassessed my life priorities after defining my driving purpose. I began by making a list of the things that were important to me. The list included faith, family, career, health, hobbies, and friends, among other things.

Although all of the things that I listed as priorities in my life were important, I wrestled with the tension between competing interests. At the time, work consumed my every waking thought. It imposed on all aspects of my life. My cell phone and email were pervasive, and I lacked the discipline to shut them down. Deadlines loomed. How could I possibly balance other priorities when the demands of my profession were so great? It was exhausting.

An honest reflection showed that my persistent focus on work to the neglect of other priorities was detrimental to my relationships, to my health, and to my soul. And though difficult to comprehend at the time, it was also detrimental to my productivity and positive impact at work. In my case "working more" was not consistent with "enhanced results." (If you're a skeptic like I was, we will revisit the bigger picture of productivity and healthy balance in other chapters of this book.)

In my effort to reassess my life and pursue a healthier balance, I asked myself some simple but tough questions relative to the pairing of each priority in my life against another priority in my life. Those questions were as follows:

- Am I willing to sacrifice <PRIORITY ONE> in favor of <PRIORITY TWO>?
- Do I sacrifice <PRIORITY ONE> in favor of <PRIORITY TWO>?

As an example, I asked myself, "Am I willing to sacrifice *family* in favor of *career*?" While there may always be instances where *career* would require focused periods of attention at the expense of my *family*, I considered the question from a much broader and more extreme perspective. In other words, if I had to pick one over the other, which would it be?

Responding to the question from the extreme perspective forces us to bring enhanced clarity to the priorities in our lives. I then asked myself the second question. In the example offered, "Do I sacrifice *family* in favor of *career*?" Recognizing that there will always be circumstances that warrant sacrifices of one priority in favor of another, I answered this question in terms of relative frequency: never, rarely, sometimes, often, or always.

I answered the two simple but powerful questions for every combination or pairing of one priority against the other. Based on my responses to the first question for each pairing, I was able to identify my professed priorities as follows:

1. Faith/Family
2. Family/Faith
3. Health
4. Career
5. Hobbies
6. Friends

My response indicated an equivalence between faith and family while acknowledging that I was *not* willing to sacrifice my faith, family, or health in favor of my career. Unfortunately, my responses to the second question for each pairing produced a different set of demonstrated priorities.

1. Career
2. Family
3. Faith

4. Health

5. Friends

6. Hobbies

The results were disturbing. My professed priorities were inconsistent with my demonstrated priorities. The hypocrisy was evident. I often sacrificed my faith, family, and all other life priorities in favor of my career. Even though I professed higher relative importance to my faith, family, and health, I didn't demonstrate this through my actions.

To be clear, don't use *time* as a proxy for determining if you sacrifice one area of your life for another. Just because I spend more time at work than I do at church doesn't mean I'm sacrificing faith in favor of my career. Rather, it's important to define what a sufficient focus is within each priority area of your life. We'll dive into this in Chapter 7.

In my case, the results were clear. I often missed church due to weekend work or simply a need to catch up on sleep. I lacked a foundation in prayer and reflection. More pervasive, I defined myself by "what I did," rather than "who I am" as part of my foundational, Christian beliefs.

Similarly, I neglected my family in favor of the persistent, and often self-imposed, demands of my job. I frequently missed dinner with the family. While I was physically present for many family events, I wasn't mentally present. On several occasions, my wife and children had to repeat questions to me because I'd tuned out everything around me. My lack of mental focus was revealed as I watched helplessly while my car, with my son inside, landed in my neighbor's front porch.

I used the exercise to state my personal definition of balance in terms of my professed priorities. Simply put, I discovered healthy life balance when I rarely sacrificed a higher professed priority item in favor of a lower professed priority item. In other words, I had healthy life balance when my professed priorities were consistent with my demonstrated behaviors.

Reflecting on your mission and what you value, I encourage you to make a list of priority areas in your life. To help you prioritize this list and to identify the conflict between your professed priorities and the priorities demonstrated in how you live your life, I've developed the *CEEK Life Balance Assessment*. As a purchaser of this book, you are authorized to take this assessment as my free gift to you. Visit www.ceekllc.com/balance for instructions on how to access and take the assessment for free.

You'll receive a personalized report detailing your professed and demonstrated priorities as well as significant sources of *Life Balance Tension* where professed and demonstrated priorities aren't aligned. It will also identify potential sources of *Slack*, where you have the opportunity to sacrifice one area of your life should urgent demands require additional time and resources in another area. The summary report will provide a *Balance Assessment Score*, comparisons to peers, and other tips and recommendations to pursue or sustain healthy balance.

The link to the *CEEK Life Balance Assessment* is also included at the end of this chapter and as a reminder in the last chapter. I encourage you to complete the *CEEK Life Balance Assessment* at any point to assist you with the exercises provided throughout the book.

With clarity of your priorities in life, you're better equipped to create a personal definition of balance. It's helpful to remember, however, that balance isn't a goal to be achieved. Rather, balance is a tension to be managed. This proactive assessment of your priorities will help you see balance in a more meaningful and measurable way. We'll build on these observations in future chapters.

It's also important to remember that your definition of balance will change depending on your life circumstances. As a bachelor in my twenties, my priorities were significantly different than those as a husband and father in my forties. So, consider how your priorities may change over time, and, as needed, repeat the *Life Balance Assessment* and . . . *CEEK a Better Way!*

Journal – Questions to Consider

- Considering my mission and core values, what are the priorities in my life (e.g., family, faith, career, health, etc.)?
- How do my demonstrated behaviors—how I live my life—align with or differ from my professed priorities?
- How have my priorities changed over time?

 Exercise – Consider a Deeper Dive

Complete the *CEEK Life Balance Assessment* (www.ceekllc.com/balance). Use the results of the assessment to define what balance means to you in terms of your commitment to the professed priorities of your life. Note your observations in your journal.

Connect your purpose to your work

Work is an important and necessary part of life for most of us. At the most basic level, our jobs provide a source of income to support ourselves and our families, and, in many cases, occupy one-half or more of our waking hours. Regardless of circumstances, our jobs have a significant impact on the quality of our life and that of those closest to us. Equally important, our jobs often correlate directly to our sense of purpose and fulfillment. In an ideal world, our job has the potential to provide inspiration and a sense of purpose.

Unfortunately, most people aren't inspired by their work. According to Gallup's *State of the American Workplace,* published in 2017, only one-third of the more than one hundred million full-time employees in the United States are *engaged* at work. Gallup defines engaged employees as those who "love their jobs and make their organization and America better every day." On the other hand, 16 percent of the workforce is actively *disengaged*, meaning "they are miserable in the workplace and destroy what the most engaged employees build." The remaining 51 percent of the workforce is not engaged. This group is simply going through the motions without real passion or purpose, just as I was. This group, which represents that largest percentage of the workforce, is what I refer to as *zombies* in the workforce.

One of the most significant factors for employee engagement is the connection the employee feels to the mission of the organization. Unfortunately, far too often we constrain the underlying meaning or purpose of our job to a generic position description. Worse yet, we may accuse the organization we serve of not having a *soul* without properly demonstrating our own.

I often share an old story that I first heard from Jonathan Bow, the lead pastor at Crosspointe Church in Cary, North Carolina. It demonstrates how individuals can connect with the mission of their job.

> A man comes upon three stonemasons who are building a church. He asks the first stonemason, "What are you doing?" He responds, "I'm laying brick." The man asks the same question of the second stonemason. He responds, "I'm

building a church." Finally, the man asks the third stonemason the same question. He responds, "I'm serving God."

Which of the three stonemasons is more inspired to do his job? Which is more engaged? Which is more likely to bring passion, creativity, and innovation to the work he does? Which is more likely to find fulfillment and peace in his life?

I once posed a similar question to one of my teams at work. This team was responsible for developing a technology solution that would enable businesses to apply for the ENERGY STAR certification and track energy consumption through the Environmental Protection Agency (EPA). In doing so, these businesses would demonstrate their commitment to helping protect the environment through energy-efficient buildings and products.

I collectively asked the team, "What do you do?" After a lengthy pause, one of our computer programmers responded that they "develop computer code in Java, HTML, .NET and other technologies."

I challenged the group a second time, asking, "But what do you *really* do?" After another long pause, one of the database developers volunteered, "We are building the ENERGY STAR Portfolio Manager application."

I acknowledged that these were both correct answers but pushed them further. Again, I asked, "What do you *really* do?" Finally, the youngest member of the team raised her hand and tentatively offered, "We protect human health and the environment."

"Exactly!" I replied.

I challenge you to define your job in terms of *why* not *what*. Ask yourself, "What are the implications?" Would this new definition change how you describe your job to friends and family? More importantly, would this new definition change how you go about your day-to-day activities at work?

While Gallup offers great suggestions for organizations and their leaders to promote enhanced engagement, they also note the potential for individuals to take matters into their own hands. While it's helpful to support an organization that offers a compelling, values-based mission that is consistent with your passion and values, such options may be limited and difficult to come by. Nonetheless, I contend that it's possible to connect a personal mission and values within most well-intentioned organizations.

As I shared in PART I of this book, I took the initiative to rewrite my job description. I aligned my job more closely with my passion and values. I sought to *inspire and empower my colleagues to be successful in their personal and professional lives.* Though I never stopped doing my day-to-day work, I reframed my job through the lens of a personal mission, values, and priorities. It fundamentally changed the way I went about my work and, ultimately, the trajectory of my career—for the better.

You don't have to work in professional services or be in a management or leadership position to transform the mindset and purpose you bring to your job. Redefining your job to align with your purpose more closely is not limited to select industries or professions.

As a graduate of the College of William and Mary, I had the distinct pleasure of knowing Ernestine Jackson. Any student who attended the college in the 1980s through 2002 knows Ernestine. She wasn't a professor, administrator, or coach. She was a cafeteria worker. Her job was to serve food.

That isn't how Ernestine defined her job. She served souls—that was her job description. For twenty-two years, she greeted every student who walked through that cafeteria line with a huge smile, personalized greeting, wise counsel, and hugs when needed. She was known for her signature greetings, "Hey, Baby!" or "Hey, Sugar!" always followed by "How's your day going?" Ernestine was a surrogate mother, counselor, mentor, and friend to thousands of students who crossed her path every year. She made everyone feel special.

At the college's 1992 graduation, students gave Ernestine a standing ovation when she received the Sullivan Award, an honor given to an employee of the college who demonstrates the spirit of love and helpfulness on campus. After suffering a stroke in 2000, students organized a benefit concert on her behalf. In 2002, the William and Mary student assembly established the Ernestine Award for dining services employees. And following her death in 2003, the Virginia Senate authored a joint resolution in celebration of the life of Ernestine Jackson.

Ernestine wrote a letter to the many students she served during her time at the college. Her inspirational approach to her job is best summed up in the closing paragraphs of that letter, which she addressed to "All My Babies."

> I remember that my whole reason for working was so that I could make a difference in somebody else's life. I never knew that was going to be my career job. When you think about the students being so far from their families—if I could help another young person find their lot in life. If I could have done that—help that person deal with one more day—deal with one more problem—find a solution to something that they thought was a mountain—that it was just a little thing—that they could just jump over that little hurdle and say, "I made it." If I could do that for someone, then I too had accomplished something. And then just to see your young, trusting eyes. . . .
>
> I always had a selfish motive for working at William and Mary—one was the children that came (they will always be children—60 years old and they are still children to me). I always focus on the kids—the students—and what would make them happy. Making them smile. Making their hearts a little less heavy. That was my main aim in coming to work. (Ernestine Jackson, pers. comm.)

Ernestine exemplifies what it means to define your job in terms of *why*, not *what*. She aligned her job to her reason for being. Her work and life were in perfect harmony . . . balanced.

As a professor of organizational behavior at the Yale School of Management, Dr. Amy Wrzesniewski and her colleagues studied the art and science of what they now refer to as "Job Crafting." They essentially define job crafting as the initiative employees take to redesign their jobs in a manner that enhances their job satisfaction and engagement at work. Job crafting is the intentional effort to capitalize on personal passion and strengths. Through related research, Dr. Wrzesniewski and her colleagues studied the cleaning crew at The University Hospital.

They discovered two distinct groups after conducting interviews and observations of the cleaning crew at the hospital.

The first group described their job in a manner consistent with their job description provided by the hospital and stated their job title as provided in that job description. They didn't perceive their job as highly skilled, and they were largely there for the pay and benefits.

The second group described a broader set of job requirements, many of which were not explicitly included in their job description. Unlike their colleagues, they viewed their job as highly skilled. They enjoyed their work. And when specifically asked about their job title, they had a variety of responses that conveyed a broader mission. Such responses included "I am an Ambassador" and "I am a Healer."

Though there were no differences between the stated job requirements of the two groups, Dr. Wrzesniewski and her colleagues observed that the second group performed tasks and services beyond that expected of them. In general, they would pay attention to the mood of the patients in the rooms they cleaned. In some cases, they would escort elderly patients back to their cars. One employee went so far as to rearrange and switch the pictures on the walls in coma patients' rooms. When she was asked why she did this, she expressed the hope that changing some aspects might spark a recovery in some way.

Dr. Wrzesniewski discovered that those who crafted their job to serve a greater purpose were more engaged, satisfied, and committed to their work. They achieved higher levels of performance and generally found greater job or career mobility.

I challenge you to find creative ways to *craft* your job to align with your purpose and values. The connection may not be obvious at first, but there are likely unique and innovative ways that you can pursue your life's purpose in most well-intentioned organizations. Consider your job in terms of *why you do it* as opposed to *what you do*. When your purpose is aligned more closely with your job, life balance becomes more attainable. You will find greater fulfillment in your job and your life.

 ## Journal – Questions to Consider

- How can I redesign my job to better align my work with my newly defined mission and/or values?
- What actions can I take to demonstrate this alignment with my mission and/or values?
- Who must I engage with and what conversations or steps must I take to facilitate the necessary changes?

 ## Exercise – Consider a Deeper Dive

Rewrite your job description in a way that connects to your personal mission statement and values. Consider defining your job in terms of *why* as opposed to *what* you do. Determine how this will change how you approach your work. Identify the rituals you can put in place that become your *signature* or what you're known for in your profession.

CHAPTER 6

BREATHE

For breath is life, so if you breathe well
you will live long on earth.

~ Sanskrit Proverb

Close the book. Close your eyes. Inhale deeply. Exhale. Repeat.

CHAPTER 7

ESTABLISH ROUTINES

Someday is not a date.

~ Dr. Phil McGraw

So, you've articulated your values and identified a purpose. You're inspired, and you better understand yourself and what's important to you. It's now time to act. Someday is today.

For many of us, our journey of self-discovery and pursuit of healthy balance ends with Chapter 5. We defined a mission and set priorities. Then what? We return to the daily grind.

As an organizational development consultant, I've seen the same trend in business. Leaders work across their teams to clarify the mission, vision, and values of the organization. Priorities are clear. Everyone leaves inspired and hopeful for the future. Then what? They return to the daily grind.

Healthy balance is defined as the "state where professed priorities are consistent with demonstrated behaviors." Now that you've stated your priorities, it's time to focus on your behaviors. What are the routine activities that you adopt to reinforce your priorities? What are those activities and rituals that restore your mental, physical, and spiritual well-being? Can you commit to these routines with the same tenacity that we seem to give to the perpetually urgent?

In this chapter, I provide guidance and examples that will help you:

1. Specify recurring rituals
2. Express your values, and
3. Sustain what's important

Healthy balance is more readily observed and attained when you identify and pursue non-negotiable activities and behaviors that reinforce your priorities and restore your spirit.

Specify recurring rituals

Years ago, I invited the teaching pastor of my church, Steve Daugherty, to speak to my team at work about balance. Steve and our lead pastor, Jonathan Bow, had been very influential in my personal pursuit of healthy life balance. They both spoke on numerous occasions on the need and value to "pause, to rest, to refuel."

They helped me recognize that I'm not defined by what I produce, but rather by the person I am and the relationships I have. I discovered a new capacity to maximize my productivity and impact at work and at home by following their helpful guidance.

Unbeknownst to me, Steve brought a full drum set to the speaking engagement. He kicked off his talk by asking if anyone knew how to play the drums. Instead of calling on someone with experience, he invited me up to demonstrate.

Since I have a limited musical background, I proceeded to bang away on the drums. I picked up the pace and volume, which was encouraged by my colleagues, finally achieving a chaotic, incoherent symphony of noise.

Steve sarcastically thanked me for my contribution and sent me back to my seat. He then demonstrated the correct way to play the drums with rhythm and melody. As he did, he noted the significance of the space between each percussive impact. He observed that while it's possible for anyone to play all the right notes, the accomplished musician understands that you must get the "spaces" or "pauses" between the notes correct in order to make beautiful music.

What kind of music are you composing in your life? Are you hitting the right notes without regard for the space between? When do you pause?

My feeble attempt at playing the drums was an apt metaphor for how I'd been living my life. I was far from an accomplished musician. The busier I got, the harder and more frequent my banging became.

From that point forward, I adopted the mantra to "honor the space between the notes" as a guiding principle and behavior statement for myself and my colleagues at work. To be clear, I don't equate this mantra to the practice of rest and recovery—although that's a critical component. Rather, we recognize non-work priorities, including rest, as the necessary and important space between the notes. You'll compose beautiful music at work and in all of life if you get the timing right.

Because I hadn't honored the space between the notes, my work was consuming my time and energy at the expense of all other priorities, including faith, family, and health. I pounded the work notes with great frequency. But the space between them was limited and not discernable amid the noise.

It took intentional action on my part to change my tune. Based on my professed priorities, and as previously detailed in Chapter 3 of this book, I took the initiative to define daily, weekly, monthly, and yearly activities that would demonstrate my commitment to each neglected priority area of my life. I included activities that fed my soul, restored my strength, and served as a reminder that I'm more than what I produce. As my longtime friend and colleague at CEEK, Jennifer Hughes, often reminds me, each of us is a human "being," not just a human "doing."

I frequently review and update my list of recurring commitments in accordance with changing circumstances of my life and tensions revealed through my own *Life Balance Assessment*. It is my intentional commitment to such recurring activities or rituals that provides me with a tangible framework upon which to define, measure, and pursue healthy balance.

While I can't profess a perfect record in regard to sustaining the daily, weekly, monthly and yearly commitments I specified in support of priority areas of my life, I'm awfully close. Without question, the commitment to such priorities renewed my faith, salvaged my family, and restored my health.

Before defining my priorities and the activities and routines that reinforce them, I lived my life without intentional design. I was easily swayed by the issue of the moment, the loudest voice in the room, the seemingly most pressing need. And because I spent a good ten hours of my day "in the office," my job was the most common distraction. It was perpetual and always urgent.

I placed my new commitments on my work and home calendars: daily exercise and dinner with the family, weekly rest on Sundays and lunch dates with my wife, monthly activities with each child, and annual vacations in the mountains, among others. I set boundaries. I honored the space between the notes.

To my surprise, I discovered that my colleagues at work were happy to adapt. The fact that I wasn't available at six o'clock in the evening wasn't an issue that worried them. The fact that I rarely responded to emails on Sundays didn't inconvenience my peers. The fact that I claimed to have no cell phone or internet access while in the mountains of Pennsylvania with my family every year seemed to be a known and appreciated white lie.

I quickly discovered that urgency in my life was often self-imposed. My impulse has always been to respond quickly, to knock things off the list, to "get 'er" done . . . *now*. While such an approach has some merit, it can be debilitating without an appropriate filter. My commitment to routines that reinforced my priorities and restored my spirit had become one such filter.

There will always be urgent demands if you let there be urgent demands. The question isn't, "How do I manage my time?" Rather, the question is, "How do I manage my commitments?" How do I manage the expectations others place on me? How do I manage the expectations that I place on myself? We'll revisit these concepts in Chapter 13.

I encourage you to review your *Life Balance Assessment* report. It's likely that this assessment revealed instances where your *demonstrated* priorities aren't consistent with your *professed* priorities. You make sacrifices in areas of your life that are more important in favor of other areas that are deemed less important. In some cases, this may be conscious and necessary. In other cases, this may be without thoughtful consideration and unnecessary.

For the *Life Balance Tensions* identified within the assessment report, create daily, weekly, monthly, and yearly routines that restore you mentally, physically, and spiritually. Put them on the calendar. Be intentional about them and be realistic about the reasonable constraints of your work schedule.

If you doubt the feasibility of sticking to the rituals that you define, ask yourself why. In most cases, you'll find that it's because of the current circumstances of your life and the priority *you* place on the commitment.

Most of us need not look any further than our past to understand why we do this. What happened when you experienced adversity at home, an illness, the loss of a loved one, a suffering child, a financial setback, a broken relationship, or some other unexpected event? Your focus likely shifted to a new priority.

In 2015, I had established a great rhythm between my faith, family, work and personal well-being activities. I was healthy, inspired, and balanced. I had what we like to call *pre-crisis* integrity. Then in November of that year, circumstances changed.

My wife had surgery on her knee, which required six weeks without bearing weight or driving. Simply put, she was out of commission. Then my daughter, a competitive gymnast, fractured her wrist prior to two out-of-town meets. My son was in the midst of three consecutive weekends of travel soccer tournaments while also kicking off a new basketball season on a team that I coached.

Needless to say, that month was chaotic. My priorities changed. Between trips to schools, doctors, physical therapists, practices, and tournaments, I had to find time to manage a full-time job while assuming greater responsibility to feed the family, prepare for the holidays, and plan an annual charity event that my company hosted.

Without pre-crisis integrity, I'm not sure I would have managed through this time. I'm quite certain that if that all had occurred before I intentionally designed my life and pursued healthy balance, I would have ended up in the hospital as well.

Instead, I was able to recognize and adapt to the temporary adversity. And in spite of the chaos and fatigue, I was grateful for the experience. It served as a clear reminder of the value my spouse brings to our family, our relationship, and my personal and professional pursuits. I couldn't sustain what I do without her.

Such circumstances will happen to all of us. At some point, your priorities and commitments will change. Your focus will shift. You'll adapt your work schedule to accommodate and adjust to a new set of priorities by changing your commitments accordingly. Hopefully, others will be there to help.

If we can change our commitments in response to a crisis, we surely can do the same when circumstances are relatively stable. Establish and commit to routines to restore the priorities in your life. Be proactive. Though periodic circumstances may warrant adjustment, they'll never happen if you aren't intentional. Honor the space between the notes.

 Journal – Questions to Consider

- What current activities in my life demonstrate a commitment to the life priorities I have identified?
- What new recurring activities would help further reinforce the professed priorities of my life?
- How might a commitment to such activities support my mental, physical, or spiritual well-being?

Exercise – Consider a Deeper Dive

For each of the *Life Balance Tensions* identified in your *CEEK Life Balance Assessment*, define at least four goals, stated as daily, weekly, monthly, or yearly commitments, that you can make to reinforce your professed priorities in life. Specify the schedule and frequency with which you commit to fulfilling each activity. As appropriate, place the specified commitments on your home and work calendars. Track your progress as a relative percentage of commitments maintained. Note your progress in your journal.

Express your values

I work with executives in many organizations in my role as a leadership coach. I often ask my clients about the priorities of their organizations. The conversation typically goes something like this:

"Is your strategy important?" "Yes," they respond. "Do you have a strategic plan." "Absolutely."

"Is growth important?" "Yes," they reply. "Do you have a sales and marketing plan?" "Of course."

"Are finances important?" "Yes," they answer. "Do you have a financial management plan?" "Sure do."

"Is your culture important?" "There is nothing more important to our success," they state proudly. "Do you have an intentional culture plan?" Silence.

Eventually, most leaders will note that they have a set of core values. They do their best to recite those values as they might appear on their website. I dig further.

How are those values revealed in the day-to-day operations of the organization? How do those values differentiate the organization in service to your colleagues, clients, and the community? What can you do to define the expected behaviors that will differentiate your organization in a manner consistent with those values? If nothing is more important than those values, doesn't it make sense to have an intentional culture plan?

In today's world of commoditized products and services, it is difficult to differentiate an organization by "what they do." Rather, the organization distinguishes itself by "how they do it." And if the *why* of the organization serves as a driving motivation for what they do, it is the *how* that serves as the key differentiator.

Several years ago, I brought Todd Durkin in to speak with my team about striving for greatness while maintaining a healthy, balanced approach in life and at work. Todd Durkin is a personal trainer, master motivator, business owner, and best-selling author. Check out Todd Durkin (www.todddurkin.com) if you seek positive inspiration; he'll change your life for the better.

I had the distinct pleasure of being a teammate of Todd's at the College of William and Mary and am proud to say he remains a friend and personal leadership coach.

In the midst of an incredibly motivational talk with our team, Todd told a story from the early days of his entrepreneurial aspirations, before he became a leading trainer of professional athletes, inspirational author, and reality TV star (check out the original season of *Strong*).

Todd was attending a fitness seminar in Denver, Colorado hosted at a Ritz Carlton. He and his wife, Melanie, had driven from their home in San Diego. When they arrived at the Ritz Carlton, a hotel employee opened the door and said, "Hello, Mr. Durkin."

Todd's first thought was, "How did they know my name?" As he and Melanie walked from their car to the front desk, other employees said, "Hello, Mr. and Mrs. Durkin." Todd and Melanie felt special; they felt like VIPs.

Todd made it a point to talk with the concierge. He had heard about the culture of the Ritz Carlton and understood that they had something called a *Customer Credo Card*. He asked the concierge about the core values written on the card and if it was true that every employee lived by these core principles, and in particular, making every guest feel special, as though they are a VIP.

"Is this true?" Todd inquired.

"Oh, absolutely," replied the concierge.

"Is it true that every day, there is a two-minute message on your voicemail or a meeting on one of the core values expressed on the card?" Todd pressed.

"Absolutely, that's a core competency of our business," he replied.

"So, you have a card?" Todd asked.

"Everyone has a *Customer Credo Card* on them at all times," said the concierge.

"Do you have one on you now?" asked Todd.

"Of course," came the reply.

"Can I see it?" Todd asked.

As the concierge shared his *Customer Credo Card*, he asked Todd why he was so interested. Todd explained that he worked in the fitness industry as a trainer, a coach, and a business owner. He confessed that service in the fitness industry sucks. Todd wanted to be the Ritz Carlton of the fitness industry. He wanted his clientele to feel special.

As he completed the check-in process, Todd feverishly attempted to memorize the ten value statements of the Ritz Carlton *Customer Credo Card*. Todd returned the card to the concierge and headed to the assigned room with his wife.

Within five minutes, there was a knock on the door. "Room service!" called the man at the door.

To Todd's surprise, a staff member entered with white gloves, towel over the arm, and silver platter in hand. Todd thought to himself, "This guy's hooking us up with food now! I love this place."

As the staff member pulled the top off the silver platter, there sat a single copy of the Ritz Carlton *Customer Credo Card*. It was a gift provided to Todd as a direct reflection of one of the core principles articulated on that card: "Always meet the unspoken needs of your client."

WOW! The Ritz Carlton had secured a customer for life.

Just as organizations distinguish themselves in the collective, expressed values and behaviors of the organization, so too can you distinguish yourself in the intentional expression of your values. What intentional rituals and routines are to your expressed priorities, intentional behaviors are to your expressed values. *If you live your life in a manner consistent with your priorities AND your values, you will more successfully manage the tension of life balance.*

At CEEK, we offer a workshop titled, "CEEK a Better Way . . . to Be ePIC." "Be ePIC" not only represents the core values of CEEK but also the impact we hope to have on every client and colleague with whom we engage. It represents embracing passion, integrity, and creativity.

We often mistakenly use the word *epic* to describe a single event. That Steph Curry buzzer-beater shot was epic. The firefighter's rescue was epic. Beyoncé's performance was epic. Epic isn't an expression reserved for one event. Instead, it's meant to be a long, poetic composition. It's meant to represent a series of achievements over an extended period.

In our context, ePIC embraces this concept of a long narrative, a good and compelling story. One can live an ePIC life through the *creative* application of their *passion* and values sustained with *integrity* over an extended period. In order to be ePIC, you must know what you care about (passion) and be true to yourself (integrity). Finally, you look for unique and differentiating ways to apply that passion (creativity).

You don't have to look hard to see examples throughout the world of how individuals express their passion and values in authentic and/or creative ways.

As a native of Pittsburgh, Pennsylvania, I am a huge fan of the Pittsburgh Steelers football team. Troy Polamalu is one of my favorite players of all time. He was known for his incredible playmaking in the secondary of the Steel Curtain and easily distinguished on the field because of his long, curly hair. In contrast to his reckless abandon and tremendous impact on the field, Troy was humble, soft-spoken, and modest. He values respect and sportsmanship and is grounded in his faith. Before and after every play, Troy made the sign of the cross on the field. This simple and often unnoticed gesture represented a direct application of his values sustained over an extended period of time. While each individual instance of this gesture was not noteworthy, its sustained application was. It was ePIC.

You don't have to be rich or famous to establish and sustain an ePIC expression of your values. The story I shared earlier of Ernestine Jackson is a perfect example of what it means to be ePIC in the persistent expression of one's values. For more than twenty years (a long, poetic narrative), Ernestine greeted every student in the most genuine and positive manner. Her greeting became her signature. It was ePIC.

As I look back on my life, the people I remember most and the ones who had the greatest impact on me all had a signature, or a compelling expression of their personal values sustained over an extended period of time. These memories include a grade school basketball referee whose calls were legendary, a crossing guard who offered a dog biscuit every day to every canine escorting a child to school, a high school teacher who affectionately called me and other students "dirtbags," and a camp director who every year sang "I'm a Little Teapot" as though hosting a rock concert.

These fun, unique, impactful, and authentic expressions of core values often become the signature by which individuals are remembered. These expressions also serve the individual as a reminder of who they are and what they care about, thereby promoting healthy balance. Their signature is a clear and readily seen expression of their values. As they're applied over time, these expressions have the tendency to transform the ordinary to extraordinary.

Thinking about your daily, weekly, monthly, and yearly rituals, what behavior or behaviors will represent an authentic expression of your core values? For what do you want to be remembered? What will be your signature?

I conclude this section with my personal expression of my values. I hope one day my family, friends, and colleagues will remember me for the challenge I place upon myself and others to "Be ePIC." This mantra will remain as a greeting I impart to all. Some will find it odd. Others might find it humorous. I don't care. Over time, it may be recognized as a unique and defining characteristic, reflecting the person that I am.

Be ePIC!

 ## Journal – Questions to Consider

- What behaviors or rituals can I adopt as a personal expression of the mission and values I've defined?
- Where and how can I apply these behaviors or rituals in my life?
- How will the persistent application of these behaviors or rituals over time make me feel?

 ## Exercise – Consider a Deeper Dive

Think of three people in your life whom you remember because of a unique and impactful behavior, greeting, mantra, etc., that they exhibited over an extended period. In your journal, document your thoughts about the values this person revealed through their repeated behavior. Now, revisit your mission and core values. Assess if your mission and values are visible to your family, friends, and colleagues through your behaviors or rituals. Identify at least one differentiating behavior or ritual that you'll adopt as a reflection of your values. Try it out for three weeks, and observe how it makes you and others feel.

Sustain what is important

Years ago, I watched my son load his backpack before heading off to school. He stuffed it with binders for math, language arts, science, and social studies. He would add a calculator, a bag for pens and pencils, and a water bottle. On some days, he stuffed his gym shoes in the side pockets and a T-shirt and shorts in any remaining space. Lastly, he fought to squeeze his lunch bag into a remaining front pocket.

After doing this daily for several weeks, the seams bulged and eventually the zipper burst. So, we got him a bigger backpack. Eventually, he found more things to put into the new backpack. Once again, the seams bulged and the zipper burst.

Is this an accurate metaphor for your life? Look in your drawers, closets, and refrigerator. Is everything filled to maximum capacity? Have you ever bought a new house to have more space, only to find the space completely filled one year later?

Does this same tendency to fill space pervade your work and life calendar? Will you burst at the seams with one more action item, calendar invite, or email request? Do pressing fires take up any intended free time? Are you able to sustain any slack in your schedule for creative or strategic thought? Or, do you sacrifice the important for the perpetually urgent?

As noted before, the identification and adoption of rituals or recurring activities that are consistent with your life priorities are critical to the pursuit of healthy life balance. However, if those activities are introduced without commitment, they may quickly succumb to an already packed schedule and the perceived crisis of the day. Unfortunately, the strategic and important often falls prey to the tactical grind and daily demands. This is just as true in our lives as it may be in the organization you serve. We routinely forgo a date with our significant other, our morning exercise routine, our dinner with family, or the private time of prayer or meditation, because there's always another job to do or person to serve.

As the saying goes, "put your oxygen mask on first." Protect your time. Be disciplined. Leave some space in your backpack. *Don't sacrifice the important for the perpetually urgent.*

In 1973, researchers at the Princeton Theological Seminary conducted an experiment known as the "Good Samaritan Experiment." The parable of the Good Samaritan, as recounted in the book of Luke 10:25–37, tells the story of a man who was attacked, beaten, and left on the side of the road by robbers. The parable tells of how a priest and a Levite, both considered spiritual elite, passed by the man without offering any help. Then a third man, a Samaritan considered of low spiritual and cultural standing, stops and tends to the man. He escorts the man to an inn where he pays the innkeeper to look after him.

The parable explains what it means to be a neighbor while suggesting that standing in society doesn't matter to God. The bigger question asked by the researchers of the Good Samaritan Experiment is, what affects our decisions to help others in need? Or more generically, what impacts our willingness to remain true to our values and beliefs?

The researchers recruited several seminary students to participate in their study. After completing a questionnaire about religious views, values, and types, the students were divided into two groups. One group was told they would need to prepare a talk about the story of the Good Samaritan as told in the Bible. The second group was told they would need to prepare a talk on careers in the seminary. As part of the experiment, the students were told that they needed to go to another building across campus to do their work.

Each student was sent on their way with varying levels of urgency. Some were told that they were already late for the next step in the process while others were given more than enough time to make it across campus to the second location. Along the route, each student would pass a man hunched over, writhing in obvious discomfort.

The study results revealed that the majority of students who weren't in a hurry stopped to help the man, while only 10 percent of the students who were rushed stopped to help. The subject matter of the task had no impact on helping behavior, nor did they find any correlation between religious types and helping behavior. Simply put, the amount of haste induced in the subject had a major impact on helping behavior. In summary, a person in a hurry is less likely to help people, even if he or she is going to talk about the parable of the Good Samaritan.

Perhaps this result seems obvious and justifiable to you. Of course, I would stop to help someone in need. However, if I'm in a hurry. . . .

The question this raises is obvious. At what point in our lives do our values become a luxury? Do you sacrifice what's important for the urgent? Do we make regrettable decisions because our values and priorities are conditional? Is this the root cause of why the employees of organizations are often susceptible to unethical behavior?

Furthermore, in the midst of your perpetual chaos, where is there time for joy? What's the consequence of your constant hurry? Does your work suffer? Do your relationships suffer? Do your *values* suffer?

In the 1950s, President Dwight D. Eisenhower introduced what has since been known as Eisenhower's Urgent/Important Principle. Stephen Covey later adopted and adapted this principle via the Time Management Matrix pitting "Urgency" of activities with the "Importance" of activities. The matrix below shows a simple way to categorize how we spend our time.

	Urgent	Not Urgent
Important	• Crying child • Work deadlines • Crises/fire	• Strategic planning • Exercise & rest • Relationships
Not Important	• Some phone calls • Some emails • Time-based offers	• Social media • Television • Busy work

Examples are provided within each of the four quadrants formed by this matrix. For instance, at the intersection of Urgent and Important, we often find imminent work deadlines or a response to an injured or upset child. Activities on the extreme opposite, such as social media, television, and busy work may be considered Not Urgent and Not Important.

Many of us live our lives in the Urgent column. Worse yet, we mistake everything in the Urgent column as falling in the Important row. That was me. For better or worse, I'm a people-pleaser. I don't want to disappoint anyone. I had an inability to say no and lacked the self-discipline and awareness to distinguish and prioritize what was important. I lived in a constant state of urgent response. It was stressful and exhausting. More importantly, as the Good Samaritan Experiment demonstrates, it put my priorities and values at risk.

Where and when did I ignore the needs of my spouse, a child, a friend, or a colleague in favor of another seemingly urgent demand? More often, where and when did I ignore my own needs for trivial or not important demands?

The answer to these questions seemed to be everywhere and always. Until I learned to distinguish between what I deemed important and what I deemed not important, I lived my life subject to the expectations of others. Until I learned to distinguish between what I deemed to be urgent and what wasn't urgent, I lived my life in a constant state of urgent response. And until I learned to say no, I would never achieve healthy life balance. Having the courage to say no to the perpetually urgent is critical to anyone's pursuit of healthy and sustainable life balance.

In his book, *The Undoing Project,* Michael Lewis shared a story about how famed Israeli psychologist Amos Tversky would only open the mail of interest to him. He would leave daily piles of unopened mail on a table, pushing them aside each day until one day's pile would reach the end of the table. Tversky would then push it off the edge of the table into the awaiting garbage can. He ended the story with an observation attributed to Tversky about things that are urgent: the longer you wait, the less urgent things become.

What things that appear urgent today, won't be urgent tomorrow? What things can you push off the table? Do you have to respond to every text message, Snapchat post, and Twitter update? Do you have to answer every call? Can you say *no* to the little things so that you might say *yes* to the big things?

I encourage you to review the list of recurring rituals and activities that you identified earlier in this chapter. If you're like me, I suspect all of those activities would fall in the Important but Not Urgent quadrant of the time management matrix. Thus, to sustain such routines, you must not only make them a priority but also rid yourself of seemingly urgent distractions. The question is how.

Years ago, I was overwhelmed in my job. I spent the majority of my day in meetings and spent evenings and weekends catching up on work that should have been done during the day. In a company of seven thousand people, anyone could view my calendar and schedule time to meet. Of course, I could decline the invite or suggest another time, but I rarely did.

So, one day I decided to block off two hours every week on my calendar. I labeled this activity as Important but Not Urgent. Though at times my colleagues tried to schedule conflicting meetings, I held my ground. I stubbornly protected my time and managed my commitments. And through the strategic and important work that I accomplished during this window, I was able to reduce the volume of needs that would otherwise have fallen in the Urgent response category. I also practiced techniques to ignore the seemingly Urgent, but Not Important. To reduce distractions, I unplugged my phone and closed my email during this window.

We've embraced and enhanced this same concept at CEEK, where we intentionally recognize our work as just another priority in life, as opposed to a counterbalance to it. All CEEK employees adopt and sustain what we refer to as Analog Time. This is a daily or weekly allotment of time during normal business hours where we understand and accept that our colleague will be offline. We're encouraged to use this time to address the Important but Not Urgent in our lives. My colleagues and I commonly use this time for exercise, meditation, prayer, rest, time with a child or significant other, or whatever fills our tank. We disconnect to reconnect. Or, as Stephen Covey puts it, we "sharpen the saw."

What can you do to ensure that you sustain what's important? How can you prioritize and commit to the activities and rituals you've defined to reinforce the priorities in your life? I encourage you to review your *Life Balance Assessment* report again as you consider these questions. Review the "Sources of Slack" section. We define slack as the potential for an individual to create time and space to pursue what's strategic but not urgent. The report indicates instances in which you're willing to sacrifice one priority area of your life in favor of another but rarely do.

I encourage you to write down your commitment to new rituals and activities that support your priorities. Leverage any sources of slack to clear the space for such commitments. Tell others about your established routines. Engage one or more accountability partners. Put your life commitments on the home *and* work calendars.

We all need that extra push, motivation, and support. Identify people who can help and actions that will hold you accountable to your pursuit of a balanced life.

Always remember, life balance is a tension to be managed, not a problem to be solved. Work, family, health, relationships, and other unexpected circumstances may require periods of intense focus. Life will throw adversity your way. It's important to challenge yourself to reinforce your priorities through stated commitments, but they must be realistic and attainable. If life circumstances prevent you from making a commitment, revise the commitment.

Journal – Questions to Consider

Refer to your core values and the behaviors or activities that you identified to support the priorities in your life.

- In what aspects of my life do I sacrifice my values or life priorities for the perpetually urgent?
- How do such actions, or inaction, affect me mentally, physically, or spiritually?
- What actions can I take to hold myself accountable to the activities and rituals that reinforce my priorities?

 Exercise – Consider a Deeper Dive

Identify a time that you sacrificed a personal value for an urgent demand. Describe the circumstances of the event. What did you do? How did you rationalize it in your mind? How did your actions make you feel in retrospect? If you had to do it all over again, what would you have done differently? Note these observations in your journal.

For each of the daily, weekly, monthly, and yearly commitments you identified earlier to support priorities in your life, define specifics to hold yourself accountable. In your journal, note the frequency, timeframe, and resources needed to fulfill the obligation. List the actions you can take or people you can engage to hold you accountable.

CHAPTER 8

WALK

An early morning walk is a blessing for the whole day.

~ Henry David Thoreau

Close the book. Put on your shoes. Step outside. Embrace nature. Take a walk.

Chapter 9

Appreciate the Moment

We are what our thoughts have made us; so take care
about what you think. Words are secondary.
Thoughts live; they travel far.

~ Swami Vivekananda

While it's great to establish and commit to a set of rituals, activities, and behaviors that support your priorities and promote healthy balance, they'll be successful only if you're fully present to them. How often is the dinner conversation background noise to the screaming monkeys in your head? What thoughts consume your mind and steal your joy? Are you unable to enjoy the moment?

I once heard a story told as an ancient Japanese proverb that perfectly illustrates this point.

A man was walking in the jungle. A tiger in the distance spotted the man. The tiger was hungry. The man began to run. The tiger pursued. The man reached a rocky slope at the edge of the jungle. As the tiger closed in, the man slid down until he reached the edge of a cliff. Before falling over the cliff, he clasped a branch of a single berry bush.

As the man hung from the bush, he watched the tiger pacing behind him, ready to eat him up. He then looked ahead at the endless abyss, ready to swallow him up. Then the man looked at the berry bush right in front of him. He noticed that it was ripe. He picked a berry and ate it. The berry was delicious.

That's the end of the story.

Within the drama of the story lies a simple and compelling message. How often do we go through life so worried about tigers behind us and cliffs ahead of us, that we miss the berry bush right in front of us?

The fulfillment, joy, or peace of activities that reinforce our life priorities is only attainable if we are mentally present to the activity. Until we learn to physically *and* mentally put aside work, stress, worry, the slights of the past, and fears of the future, we'll never discover healthy life balance. So, silence the cell phone, shut down the email, and focus on some practical steps to improve your presence in the moment.

This chapter provides some helpful guidance and examples that will help you:

1. Become more mindful
2. Put the balls down, and
3. Live in the moment

As you'll soon discover, balance is more readily discovered when you're present to the many blessings of your life.

Become more mindful

A simple online search will tell you that typical humans have anywhere from fifty- to seventy-thousand thoughts per day. However, in my own research, I've struggled to find credible and authoritative sources for these assumptions. Various references to National Science Foundation research claim that the average person has anywhere from twelve- to sixty-thousand thoughts per day.

While these estimates vary widely, it's safe to say that we are thinking beings. Thoughts come into and go out of our minds at a rapid rate. Assuming eight hours of sleep per day, we average approximately one thought every second on the high end, and one thought every five seconds on the low end. Regardless of the estimate, that's a lot of thinking.

There also seems to be considerable research that attempts to estimate the nature of our thoughts. Once again, I find some variance in the research and associated literature. However, it seems that most articles reference the notion that approximately 70 to 80 percent of our thoughts, on average, are negative thoughts. Furthermore, research seems to suggest that as much as 98 percent of our thoughts are repetitive. In other words, we revisit the same negative thoughts in our mind—over and over again.

Stop reading for a moment. Simply sit in silence with your thoughts for the next sixty seconds.

. . .

How many different thoughts entered your mind?

Did any thoughts repeat? Did you have the same thought earlier today?

How many thoughts were negative? How many were positive?

Did you think this was a silly exercise with no redeeming value and simply continue reading? Guess what? That too was a negative thought.

It's not always easy to distinguish what some might call "unique and independent thoughts." I'm guessing you had several thoughts pop in and out of your mind. While you may not categorize all of your thoughts as negative, can you say that any were overwhelmingly positive?

As a side note, this is the point in this book's original manuscript where I did a considerable amount of research. I intended to reference a number of recent studies on mindfulness, our brains, and the power of our thoughts. I set out to "WOW" you with my knowledge of the latest science. The universal response from early reviewers of my book was that I lost my voice and ultimately the attention of the reader.

Upon honest reflection, my original approach to this section was largely driven by recurring negative thoughts. "Who am I to speak to others about mindfulness and the power of our thoughts?" "What makes me credible?" After considering the valued feedback I'd received, I put those thoughts to bed and surrendered my need to be perceived as an authority on this topic.

If the latest research on the power of mindfulness is what you want, I encourage you to search online for mindfulness, positive psychology, or the power of thoughts. You'll find plenty of compelling and relevant studies. However, I can save you the trouble. It's been proven that your thoughts have a significant impact on your mental, physical, and spiritual well-being. As we explore later in this chapter, positive thoughts are associated with lower levels of depressed mood, anxiety, and stress. Positive thinking enhances productivity and problem-solving capabilities. Positive thinking has been shown to influence physical health and recovery.

While there seems to be a general consensus regarding the power of our thoughts, the bigger and more elusive question is, what control do you and I have over our thoughts? Can I consciously choose to keep certain thoughts from entering my head, or am I simply subservient to the thoughts that subconsciously come and go?

While I can't answer such questions with authority, I can speak from practical experience.

I concede that I may not be able to prevent a negative thought from entering my head at any given point in time; however, I do have tremendous power to influence my thoughts—and so do you.

The ability to influence thoughts is where meditation and mindfulness offer tremendous potential. Research has shown what Buddhists have known for centuries: meditation and mindfulness decrease anxiety and stress, regulate emotions, enhance cognitive functions, and improve general health and wellness.

I've tried to build a meditation practice into my daily routine with mixed results. Unfortunately, I haven't found much success in using meditation to quiet my mind. Instead, I've found success in using meditation to bring greater clarity to the nature of my thoughts. Rather than leverage the discipline to quiet my mind, I embrace the quiet solitude to let my heart and soul speak, to let the thoughts come and go as they may. In doing so, I enhance my awareness of the fears, anxiety, or insecurities that may be weighing on me. Meditation was particularly helpful in identifying and overcoming my tendency to seek affirmation from others. It also exposed the irrational anxiety and stress caused by my perceived assessment of others' reactions to me or my work.

I encourage you to get comfortable with silence. Sit still. Just be. Let your thoughts come and go as they will. Don't judge your thoughts. Simply build awareness. Note the pervasive thoughts that occupy the space between your ears. Take an inventory of the predominant nature of your thoughts. Being intentionally aware of your most common thoughts is the only way for you to know if you're successful in controlling your thoughts.

Now, if you're like me, sitting in silence and examining your thoughts may seem odd. It's different and can be uncomfortable. Like anything, it takes practice. Nonetheless, I encourage you to consider daily meditation, prayer, or other mindfulness techniques as a way to enhance awareness and calm your mind, body, and spirit.

Perhaps you're skeptical of the power of these practices to build awareness and ultimately influence the nature of your thoughts. That's okay. Let's suspend that notion for now. Instead, consider for a moment what influences your thoughts. I think we can all agree that what comes out of our minds is largely influenced by what goes into our minds.

We're a product of what we consume. The thoughts that we hold and the behaviors we exhibit are strongly influenced by the information we absorb. In most cases, we're simply not aware of the impact our information consumption has on our thoughts, opinions, behaviors, and general disposition.

Consider these questions:

- What books do you read?
- What news do you take in?
- What music do you listen to?

- What shows or movies do you watch?
- What magazines do you subscribe to?
- What Twitter, Facebook, Snapchat, or Instagram accounts do you follow?
- What people do you engage with and listen to?

Our brains are like sponges, absorbing those things we watch, listen to, and read—even if we do those activities mindlessly. What we take in, eventually comes out. It's the theory behind marketing and propaganda. Just like the water that releases from the sponge, so too will the thoughts, words, actions, or behaviors release when you apply stress or pressure to the mind, the body, or the soul.

If you want to influence your thoughts in a positive manner, be aware of what you consume.

Social media is probably the most relevant example of our day. While tools like Facebook offer a great mechanism to keep up with friends and family, researchers have studied the psychological impact of access to such sources of information. Excessive use of social media has been linked to depression, envy, and a general decline in health and well-being because it taps into basic human nature: the need to compare ourselves to others. We understand this intuitively. We compare our lives, our children, our bodies, our income, our experiences, our fitness, and our things. This kind of comparison is a surefire way to hit and exceed the national statistics regarding the percentage of negative thoughts that consume our attention. Comparison is the enemy of contentment.

When was the last time you posted the video of your two-year-old child throwing a temper tantrum? Did you update friends on your latest trip to a local fast-food restaurant? How about that video of your child giving up the game-winning goal? Or, are you the one who posted the update of the weight you gained over the holidays and the jeans that no longer fit?

No. More commonly, we post pictures from the exotic vacation, of the new car, or the fancy night on the town. We glorify the exceptional moments of our children—the game-winning shot or another semester of straight A's. Our posts most often project the extraordinary life in lieu of the ordinary.

Nothing's wrong with such updates. The question is, as the consumer of this information, what thoughts occupy your mind? Are you happy for your friends and colleagues? Or do you envy or resent them?

If you're not content or fulfilled in your life, you're more susceptible to the comparison trap. Externally, you may congratulate your friends, "like" their posts, and tell them you're happy for them. Internally, you tell yourself, "must be nice." Perhaps you craft another story in your mind—one that delegitimizes the source of another's success. Do you find it difficult, if not impossible, to feel true joy for another's good fortune?

I fundamentally believe that comparison is the most destructive, optional force relative to our thoughts. While I characterize our tendency to compare as an "optional" force, I recognize that mental illness and disease can have a debilitating effect on one's mind and spirit. I acknowledge that those circumstances may impact an individual's tendency to compare and be out of the individual's direct control. However, for most of us, comparison is a choice we make that robs us of joy.

Years ago, Jeff Manion spoke at our church. Jeff is the author of *Satisfied: Discovering Contentment in a World of Consumption.* He shared a simple but compelling story about the impact of comparison. A father gave a child a scoop of ice cream. He noted how happy the child was with his scoop of ice cream. Everything was good.

Then the father gave two scoops of ice cream to a second child.

Enough said. You get where this story is going. Of course, it's a good thing we grow out of this as adults. Surely, we wouldn't throw a fit if someone else gets a little more than we do. Or would we?

For many years, I suffered because of my tendency to compare. When I was young, I sought to be bigger, stronger, and faster like the athletes I admired. Like many teenagers, I sought to fit in and belong. I was aware of what I had and what I didn't have. I sought to enhance my resume relative to my peers. I wanted the better job and higher income, not because I was inspired, but because I might rank higher than others. I compared how much I was valued by others relative to my peers. It was superficial and exhausting.

With help and a willingness to dig deep, I built greater awareness. I acknowledged my thoughts. I looked for a better way. I decided that I'd no longer compare myself to others. I can honestly say, I don't care what others are doing relative to myself. For me, this freedom from comparison and the associated negative thoughts was made possible by a deeper understanding of my faith in God. I am loved and accepted. I need no further affirmation.

I am content because I no longer compare. And I no longer compare, because I am content.

In this chapter, I have stressed the impact of comparison because I believe it is the most significant factor influencing thoughts that are counter to fulfillment, peace, and healthy life balance. While comparison may be at the root of many negative thoughts, I acknowledge other sources exist that may contribute to fear, anxiety, or even undesirable behaviors.

I recently observed the negative impact the nightly news was having on my thoughts. It was causing fear about what disaster may be looming and anxiety about what I believed to be the right approach to values-based leadership. I cut back on the nightly news.

I'm an annual subscriber to *Sports Illustrated*. Several years ago, I saw my five-year-old daughter looking at the cover of the swimsuit edition. I realized at that moment that my consumption of this information wasn't good for the self-esteem I hoped to build in my daughter, nor for the respect I wanted to show to my wife. I've declined to receive that issue ever since.

Through these and several other intentional decisions, I've replaced the sources of negative thoughts with positivity. I regularly listen to inspirational podcasts. I read uplifting books with compelling life stories. I meditate and pray. I pursue my passions and interests because it's who I am, not what I think someone wants me to be.

I know it can be difficult to avoid negativity in the midst of the twenty-four-hour news cycle. If you desire to be an informed and caring citizen, you simply can't ignore the news. However, you can always find a source of light in the darkness. In the words of the famous children's television personality, Fred Rogers: "When I was a boy, and I would see scary things in the news, my mother would say to me, 'Look for the helpers. You will always find people who are helping.'"

Look for the helpers. Seek the positive in your life and that of others. Become more mindful. Build awareness of what generates stress, anxiety, or fear and what promotes joy, peace, and fulfillment. Reduce your exposure to the sources of negative thoughts and increase your exposure to sources of positivity. Observe the impact your choices have on your fulfillment and pursuit of healthy balance.

 Journal – Questions to Consider

- What sources of information do I consume on a regular basis?
- How does the repetitive consumption of this information influence my thoughts throughout each day?
- How do such thoughts impact the demonstration of my defined values and professed priorities?

 Exercise – Consider a Deeper Dive

Make a list of those "things" that you consume or that influence your thoughts on a recurring basis (music, media, news, people, places, circumstances, and other things). Observe and note in your journal the impact those things have on your thoughts, mood, and energy. Build awareness. Mentally commit to acknowledging the thoughts that arise when you experience these things. Don't judge these thoughts. Simply acknowledge them and write down your observations.

Put the balls down

As you build awareness of your thoughts, you may soon discover other patterns. Perhaps you notice that one priority area of your life takes up the majority of your mental attention regardless of where you are or what you're doing. In my case, my work occupied the majority of my thoughts.

While it's helpful to plan, schedule, and follow through on commitments and activities to restore your priorities, it's not enough to only be physically present for such priorities. As a matter of fact, it's often worse to engage in priority activities where you're physically present but mentally checked out. Such was my case.

When my children were young, my wife went out to dinner with friends. I encouraged the evening out and assured my wife that I would forgo the usual evening work to focus my attention on the kids. After dinner, we hit the playroom for some fun and games. We built a tent in the playroom. The kids dressed me like a princess. And every now and then, the kids entertained me with the latest knock-knock joke.

My daughter said, "Knock, knock."

"Who's there?" I replied.

"I've got to gope," she responded.

"I've got to gope who?" I played along.

In the midst of her laughter, she warned her brother, "Look out! Pappa has to go poo!"

Such shenanigans temporarily kept my focus. Of course, my Blackberry (am I dating myself?) was connected to my hip the entire time, and I lacked the self-discipline to ignore the ding of an incoming message. Before long, I became engrossed in the latest chain of emails while the kids were building a wall of wood bricks.

Once again, my daughter eagerly sought my participation in another knock-knock joke.

"Knock, knock," she said. She tried again after no response. "Knock, knock!" she implored.

Silence.

Finally, after a third attempt, I looked up from yet another tedious work email and impatiently shouted, "Who's there?!"

"Not Pappa," she passively replied.

That stung.

A couple of months later, the lead pastor of my church, Jonathan Bow, confessed to a nearly identical story during a personally impactful sermon. As he shared his story, it sent chills through my spine as I relived the incident with my daughter. At the same time, it was reassuring to learn that I wasn't alone. Heck, even the pastor of my church can be consumed by the constant push of information or other self-imposed pressures. Perhaps the problem was more common than I realized.

I've come to acknowledge that if my child is attuned to my lack of presence, I have a problem. I'm not living a life consistent with what I've deemed to be most important. And while I may be physically present, I might as well be on the other side of the world.

More recently, my kids caught me in yet another example of "missing the berry bush" in front of me. Our family has a black Labrador mutt affectionately known as Moxie. For the past eight years, Moxie has become ingrained in the fabric of our family. Our love for our dog is captured in one of our family behavior statements that further serves as a reflection of our values: "even the dog has a voice."

Through this statement, we honor Moxie as another member of the family that we all love and support. And, as my children will attest, I perhaps take it too far when I speak on behalf of Moxie (in my best dog voice) as though I fully understand her thoughts and aspirations.

Unfortunately, through my interactions with Moxie, my children observed another potential flaw in my pursuit of healthy balance. As a good dog owner, I often take Moxie out for exercise. I always figured, the faster I ran, the more exercise she would get *and* the quicker I could return to other, "more important" tasks.

When I took the dog for a walk or run, it seemed that my mind was always focused on work or other "things" that I needed to do. I would grow increasingly frustrated every time Moxie stopped to pee, met another dog, or simply smelled the roses. This frustration revealed itself quite clearly when in the midst of trying desperately to get Moxie to move, I shouted, "Dammit . . . you're slowing my life down."

Having overheard me, my kids laughed at the ridiculous nature of my comment. To this day, they won't let me live that one down. In the midst of their laughter, I realized the absurdity of the statement. And instead of condemning my dog, perhaps gratitude is in order. Perhaps I need to stop and smell the roses. Couldn't I sacrifice twenty minutes for a peaceful walk with the dog?

It's amazing to me how intuitive children are. Or perhaps, it's that they're more honest and direct. How many times am I mentally checked out in a conversation with a friend, colleague, or even my spouse? I'm now so aware of the behavior and signs that someone isn't present in a conversation. Unfortunately, it's a pervasive problem. Maybe the issue is less about effective listening skills and more about bad habits relative to healthy life balance, or an inability to silence and open the mind.

When I speak to organizations about healthy life balance, I typically demonstrate the concepts with a juggling metaphor. I use a set of tennis balls to represent my life priorities. They're labeled as faith, family, work, health, hobbies, and friends.

I share a generalized story of my life that typically goes something like the following.

After I graduated from college, I picked up the *work* ball. I took off with it on a dead sprint. However, I was living with my college *friends* and desired fun while sustaining those relationships. And I had various sports-related *hobbies* that I wanted to pursue. I played basketball, ice hockey, and softball, among other activities.

(As I tell the story, I begin to juggle one, two, and then the three balls introduced into my life.)

For a while, this seemed manageable. However, I realized I had lost my way in some respects. I was raised in a strong faith environment but hadn't been consistent in that practice since leaving home. So, I brought *faith* back to my life.

(I am now struggling to juggle four balls but managing.)

Suddenly, some of my activities seemed to be in conflict. The juggling got harder. So, I put aside my *hobbies* and restored some order. But I valued fitness and *health* and lost that outlet through my hobbies. So, I exercised in solitude to sustain my health.

(Again, juggling becomes difficult as I return to four balls.)

So, I decided to spend less time with *friends*. But then I missed them. Thus, I sacrificed my faith, which seemed to restore some order.

Then something crazy happened. One of my friends became a really good friend. I fell in love with her. A couple years later, I married her and started a *family*. And I wasn't going to start a family without *faith*.

And what about me and my *hobbies*? I didn't like all the sacrifices I had to make. Surely, I could find time for an occasional round of golf.

(At this point, I am attempting to juggle all six balls.)

Not surprisingly, I dropped the balls. Well, not all of the balls. I held onto one: the *work* ball.

I used to carry the *work* ball with me everywhere I went. It was pervasive. It defined who I was. I carried that ball while watching my children. I carried that ball while walking my dog. I carried that ball at dinner with my wife. I carried that ball Sunday morning at church (if I could spare the time to go). I carried that ball when socializing with friends.

The single most significant step in my pursuit of healthy balance was learning to put the work ball down and replace it with something more significant.

I started small at first and progressed over time. Initially, I would recite various mantras as I opened the garage door after driving home from work.

"My work is complete. It's time to embrace the presence of my family."

Or, "What's unfinished today is better solved tomorrow. Be present."

Or, I would simply inquire aloud about the day that my wife, daughter, son, and even the dog had experienced.

This simple habit was instrumental in shifting the focus from being self-centered to other-centered. As a result, I became more engaged with my family and less consumed by the demands of my job, which were always there.

Through these and other established routines in which I physically disconnect from the phone, email, computer, etc., I'm able to be more present to other priorities in my life. More importantly, I stopped defining myself by my job. Instead, I began defining my value by the person I am.

The ball you carry with you is the ball that defines you. The ball you carry with you becomes a personal measure of your value.

If you're an athlete, and your athletic training and events permeate nearly all aspects of your life, you'll define your value by the level of success you have as an athlete, or the perception others have of you as an athlete.

If you're a musician, and your musical competence and accomplishments permeate all aspects of your life, you'll define your value by your level of success as a musician, or the perception others have of you as a musician.

If you're a parent, and your child-rearing and children's activities permeate nearly all aspects of your life, you'll define your value by your level of success as a parent, or by the perceptions others have of your children and you as a parent.

If you're a (fill in your profession), and your profession permeates nearly all aspects of your life, you'll define your value by your level of success as a (fill in your profession), or by the perceptions others have of you as a (fill in your profession).

What *ball* do you carry with you most often? Is that the ball you want to define you? Does that ball detract from your presence to other priorities in your life? Does that ball rob you of the potential joy of other aspects of your life?

Using the juggling metaphor allowed me to establish routines and rituals that enabled me to mentally put one ball down in order to pick up another (more on that in the section to follow). More importantly, I came to realize that I have two hands. I can carry two balls.

I decided that it's perfectly acceptable to carry one ball with me at all times. With the second hand, I can always carry a second ball. The ball I choose to carry with me is a consistent and authentic representation of the person I am and what I value.

If the ball that I carry with me defines my value, what ball would I choose? After some reflection, I decided to carry a different ball. I chose to carry the *faith* ball. I was raised on a Christian foundation. I've come to understand that God's love is unconditional. I've come to own that I don't need to earn God's acceptance. In kind, I have come to accept and love myself just the way I am. I no longer compare. I no longer worry about the perception of others. I'm at peace with who I am.

To be clear, I'm not suggesting that you have to be a man or woman of faith to pursue healthy life balance effectively. I am suggesting that you consciously assess who or what defines your value. In lieu of *faith*, maybe it's the personal values that you carry with you. In that case, the ball you carry is called *values*, an alternative label for the faith ball. In my case, my values reflect my faith. And, my faith reflects my values. Regardless, your values are an authentic representation of who you are and what you care about.

One day, someone else will hold your job. One day, you won't run as fast or jump as high. Another musician will be the next great thing. But no one else will be the father, mother, brother, sister, uncle, aunt, friend, or colleague that you are. No one else will be the unique combination of talents and values that define you.

As I transition from various roles and activities in my life, I often remind myself that I'm defined by my faith and my values. As I transition from work to home, I mentally set the *work* ball aside. As I transition from home to play basketball with friends, I mentally set aside the *family* ball. All the while, I carry with me an authentic expression of my faith and values. I bring genuine interest in the successes, failures, dreams, and fears of my colleagues, family, and friends. I'm a consistent and authentic expression of the person I'm meant to be.

Establish the discipline to put down the balls that aren't relevant to the present situation. Put them aside and pick them up again at the appropriate time. Don't carry work with you everywhere you go. Similarly, learn to focus on work when at work. In doing so, you'll be more productive at work and in life, achieving greater balance along the way.

Be intentional about what you carry with you and where you carry it. The activities that promote healthy balance are only successful if we are mentally present to them. Be mindful. Be present.

Journal – Questions to Consider

- What *ball* do I carry with me most often?
- How does this tendency affect my joy or appreciation of the other priorities in my life?
- What warning signs exist that I'm carrying too many balls at once?

 Exercise – Consider a Deeper Dive

Define a mental exercise (e.g., a mantra, self-reminder, meditation, etc.) to symbolically put down any balls that impose on the activities you identified in support of other life priorities. Practice this mental exercise over the course of three weeks. Observe and write down in your journal the impact of this exercise on your focus, productivity, relationships, and general fulfillment.

Live in the moment

Several years ago, while my wife was out of town, I experienced what I'm sure single parents go through every day. I had to shuttle kids between numerous activities while squeezing work and other commitments into an already packed schedule. In between activities, I ran to a local establishment to pick up some food. I placed my order at the drive-through, paid at the window, and rushed home. I was halfway there before I realized that the only thing I'd received from the attendant was my receipt. I'd left without the food!

In my haste to get home and my preoccupation with work and kids' activities, I simply lost my focus in the moment. Though somewhat embarrassing, this isn't such a big deal when simply picking up food. However, the important question to ask is, where else do I fail to be *present* when consumed by other *baggage,* and what's the impact?

Have you attended meetings so preoccupied that you can't recall the content of the discussion? Is the dinner conversation just background noise as you solve the latest business problem? Can you recall what you read on the previous page of this book? Are you unable to live in the moment?

Via the questions and exercises presented earlier in this chapter, you hopefully enhanced your awareness of the thoughts that fill your mind and established some rituals or routines to help you put down the ball or balls that invade other aspects of your life. You're now prepared to discover what it means to live in the moment—to be present. As you engage in activities that restore your mind, body, or spirit, they will only be successful if you're mentally present to them.

I recently had a conversation with a friend during the halftime of a local basketball game. His son is a great student-athlete, and I knew he had a strong desire to compete in college. I complimented the game his son was having and asked about his college search.

My friend explained the various colleges that had reached out to his son. He told me about the recruiting conversations that had occurred and the college visits that were planned. I asked him which college his son liked the most. He explained further and shared frustrations about a school his son was keenly interested in that wasn't sufficiently showing interest in his son. Nonetheless, he expressed optimism about the array of options his son would likely have.

He then asked about my daughter and her college search.

As this friend knew, my daughter is a competitive gymnast who also aspired to compete in college. As I began to explain how she had reached out to the coaches of some schools of interest, my friend looked away. Something else clearly caught his attention. While I fully recognize that people can be preoccupied, I was taken aback by the blatancy of not only mentally checking out but also the physical indifference expressed by turning his body and looking in the opposite direction. I continued to share the specifics of my daughter's story, but it was clear that my answer to the seemingly genuine question was falling on deaf ears.

I understandably assumed that my friend had no interest in my response or my daughter, for that matter. If this became a repeated pattern, his behavior would certainly cause me to question the nature and value of the friendship. Is this the type of friend that I desire?

These observations caused me to reflect on my journey toward balance as well as the role presence has played. In the past, I know that my preoccupation with work demands, insecurities, or even the unconfirmed perceptions that I held of others, revealed itself in a lack of presence. I often asked questions of friends, family, and colleagues when I had no interest in their response. While I'd like to think that I truly cared, I was too preoccupied and self-centered to engage with anything beyond superficial interest. I was playing the game in accordance with some accepted social norms. My wife was the person who most often pointed out my lack of presence because she frequently engaged in one-sided conversations with a brick wall—me.

While I don't profess to be perfect, I'm much more intentional about living a life in the present moment. Conversations with colleagues are one simple yet incredibly impactful example. I continue to practice what it means to experience life firsthand with others. I often tell myself that there is no "one" or no "thing" more important than the individual I'm about to engage with in conversation or life.

> *There is no greater gift that you can give to another than genuine presence . . . than undivided attention in your engagement with another human being.*

I'm sure you have experienced situations similar to the one that I described with my friend. How did it make you feel? How did it affect your relationship with that individual?

Don't judge such thoughts or the individual. Rather, internalize that feeling and reflect on its application with respect to the Golden Rule—treat others as you would like to be treated. How can you practice true presence in service to others? How can you practice true presence in service to yourself?

One of the greatest inventions of our time is probably also the single greatest detriment in our efforts to live in the present moment: the cell phone. We've all seen it: waiting for the bus, standing in the elevator, taking the ten-minute meeting break, or simply appearing to be engaged when we have no one to engage.

Worse yet, we're conditioned like Pavlov's dog. We jump at the ding of a new text message. Our email is always open. We're programmed to receive instantaneous news alerts and sports updates. We're addicted to Facebook, Snapchat, Instagram, and Twitter. We *must* answer every phone call.

In April 2017, Adrian F. Ward and coauthors from the McCombs School of Business at the University of Texas released a study suggesting that even the mere presence of one's smartphone significantly reduces cognitive capacity. In their study, Ward and his colleagues had nearly eight hundred participants take a variety of tests on a computer. These tests, intended to measure cognitive capacity, required complete concentration in order to score well. All the participants were randomly instructed to place their smartphones face down on the desk, in their pocket or personal bag, or in another room. In addition, all participants turned their phones to silent.

Even without the typical distraction of active smartphones, the researchers found that the mere *presence* of the smartphone impacted cognitive performance. Those with their smartphones in another room significantly outperformed those with their cell phones on the desk in front of them. In subsequent studies, Ward and his colleagues further discovered that it really didn't matter if the cell phone was turned on or off. Simply its presence impacted performance.

These research insights are the motivation behind why my company, CEEK, adopts Analog Time as a weekly ritual. This is an intentional effort to focus on what's Important but not Urgent. We're encouraged to remove all digital technology and other physical and mental distractions.

When and where in your life can you put the smartphone away? When and where in your life can you put distractions in another room? How and when can you practice and embrace Analog Time?

I have a friend and neighbor with whom I share a mutual interest in Pittsburgh's professional sports teams. He will often text me during a Steelers or Penguins game, offering some insightful analysis or, more commonly, some frustrated rant. His messages typically include a comment about how he looks forward to my response in the year to come.

While I hope my friend doesn't perceive my common lack of responsiveness as a reflection of our friendship, I'm somewhat proud that this is how he and others see me. I love watching Steelers games with my children, whom I have sufficiently brainwashed to root for the black and gold. Isn't it a good thing that I'm not connected to my smartphone during such experiences?

In chapter 7 Establish Routines, I shared a list of recurring activities and rituals that I defined and pursued as an intentional effort to reinforce my priorities. I challenged you to create a similar list for the priorities in your life. As noted in the introduction of this chapter, the fulfillment, joy, or peace of activities that reinforce our life priorities is only attainable if we're mentally present to the activity.

For each of the activities and rituals that I defined, I made the commitment to be fully present to the activity. I quickly realized that not a single one of the activities required access to my smartphone or computer, so I physically removed them during these activities.

While this physical act is significant, it still remains difficult to ignore the screaming monkeys in my head. I won't pretend that my mind doesn't ever wander during conversations with others or while engaging in activities that support my wellness and life balance. However, the simple act of acknowledging these thoughts has been highly effective. My awareness gives me the chance to remind myself to shift my focus, to be present.

My efforts regarding presence have enhanced my personal balance and appreciation of priority activities, and my effectiveness and productivity in my career. I have spent most of my career as a consultant in technology and business. As a consultant, I'm a problem solver. I'm always looking for ways to improve my service and help my clients be successful.

More recently, I became a certified leadership coach. In this capacity, my role is less about solving problems for my clients and more about helping my clients discover their capacity to solve their problems. Admittedly, I struggled early on with this mind-set shift. I often resorted to old consulting habits in conversations with coaching clients. I continued to use language such as "I recommend that you—" or "Why would you do—" Worse yet, I often formulated intended responses or suggestions for my clients before I even heard the details of the issue or challenge they were facing.

I soon discovered that this tendency to resort to such solutions wasn't driven by a genuine interest in my client. Rather, it was driven by a desire to be valued. It was self-centered rather than other-centered.

I have since learned to enter coaching conversations with a clean slate. I come with no preconceived notions or solutions. I bring a beginner's curious mind-set. I ask lots of tough but thoughtful questions, driven by a genuine interest to learn more. In doing so, I relieve myself of the pressure to have all the answers or to be the expert in the room. I engage with clients on a more human level. As a result, I better succeed in empowering my clients to solve their problems. I attribute my success to my improved ability to be present in the moment, to put aside preconceived notions, insecurities, or other mental stressors.

I encourage you to assess where and when you're distracted from the present moment. How do such distractions detract from your productivity and the quality of your relationships? What physical and mental actions can you take to enhance your presence to activities and people that support your life priorities and balance?

Just like we do at the airport, so many of us choose to carry our baggage with us everywhere we go. It's important to establish routines and the discipline to quiet the mind and give the gift of presence to your colleagues, friends, family, and yourself. Even if it costs a little extra—check your baggage! Be here, be now, be present. You'll notice details and build relationships like never before. And, you won't have to make a second trip to the local drive-through.

 Journal – Questions to Consider

- Under what circumstances (where, when, and how often) do I find myself mentally distracted from conversations, tasks, or other activities?
- How do these distractions affect my general productivity?
- How do these distractions affect my relationships?

Exercise – Consider a Deeper Dive

Write about a recent scenario in which you weren't fully present in the moment. Describe the impact that your lack of focused attention or appreciation of the moment had on your productivity or a relationship. Alternatively, identify a recent scenario in which you were fully present in the moment. Similarly, describe the effect of focused attention on your productivity, relationship, and personal fulfillment. Decide on three things you can do physically (e.g., put cell phone away, move to a new space, etc.) or mentally (e.g., additional mantra, meditation, etc.) to enhance your presence in activities that will reinforce your life priorities and the most important relationships in your life.

CHAPTER 10

REST

*Rest is not idleness, and to lie sometimes on the grass
under trees on a summer's day, listening to the murmur of
the water, or watching the clouds float across the sky,
is by no means a waste of time.*

~ John Lubbock

Close the book. Lie down. Shut your eyes. Rest.

CHAPTER 11

CHOOSE YOUR DISPOSITION

*When I was 5 years old, my mother always told me that
happiness was the key to life. When I went to school, they
asked me what I wanted to be when I grew up. I wrote
down 'happy.' They told me I didn't understand the assignment, and I told them they didn't understand life.*

~ Anonymous

So, you defined a values-based mission or purpose. You determined the priorities in your life and established routine activities
that reinforce those priorities. You're committed to being present
as you pursue these activities. You'll do your best to live in the
moment.

The question now is, how will you show up?

Every day and every moment of your life, you have a choice to
make. Will you be an energy giver or an energy taker? Or, as the late
Dr. Randy Pausch explained in *The Last Lecture*, are you the bouncy
Tigger or the despondent Eeyore? If you can choose to accept circumstances for what they are, assume responsibility for your reactions,
and embrace a generally positive disposition, you will lead a more
peaceful and balanced life.

Your general disposition is a choice that affects you and those nearest
you. This chapter provides simple steps to build awareness and make
better choices by helping you:

   1. Observe your reactions

2. Assess your disposition

3. Take the CONN

As you will soon discover, balance is more readily achieved when you show up with a favorable disposition and optimistic outlook.

Observe your reactions

A couple of years ago, I was asked to facilitate a workshop for a group of EPA employees in Washington, D.C. In addition to facilitating a strategic planning discussion, I was planning a brief team building discussion and exercise related to general communications and the effect of our reactions in the workplace. I was excited about the opportunity to share some of my experiences about how I successfully changed some habits. I had learned over time how my constant push for progress often revealed itself through impatient reactions to anything that slowed my or my team's progress. I had discovered that my reactions, under those circumstances, were a choice that I made. Furthermore, I learned that these reactions impact me, my colleagues, and those closest to me.

I decided to leave early from my home in North Carolina so that I could make it to the hotel with enough time to complete my preparations for the workshop. Of course, I should have anticipated the nearly one-hour delay as I approached and navigated the D.C. beltway. That was the least of my problems.

After checking into my hotel, I realized that I had forgotten a belt. It was nearly 7:00 p.m., and I also needed to eat dinner. I decided to drive to the Crystal City Mall, which was approximately one mile from the hotel. I was confused by the parking options but eventually found the correct entrance to an underground garage. I pushed the button, took the ticket, and parked my car near one of the mall entrances.

I made my way to a well-known department store and found the area where men's belts were located. I found a suitable option on a table marked with a 40 percent discount. "That was easy," I thought. I went to the closest register where four employees were chatting.

I stood and waited for at least a minute. No one acknowledged my presence. I finally asked if someone could help me. With no explanation, I was instructed to find another register.

I found a second option, and the employee told me that I couldn't check out there. Again, he provided no explanation. I continued to wander the store until I found a lady behind a third register. She said she could only sell glasses there.

By now, I was officially frustrated. My heart had begun to race. My response to each subsequent employee took a more direct and disgusted tone.

I made my way to customer service. I informed the nice young lady that her store sucks. I explained that all I wanted to do was pay for a belt and get out of their awful establishment. In spite of my rudeness, she offered to "ring me up" right there.

That was nice until I discovered that she didn't apply the 40 percent discount to the sales price. So, I explained that she needed to correct the price. She checked the system. It disagreed. She asked me to show her where the belt discount was advertised.

I trekked to the other side of the store and showed her the table with the discounted belts. She shrugged, proceeded back to her customer service desk, and promptly completed the transaction with a 40 percent discount. I sarcastically suggested that she change the name of her desk.

I then left the department store in search of food. I spotted the food court directly below me, but the only way down was to walk halfway across the mall to the only available escalator.

My blood pressure rose higher.

I finally reached the food court and decided to eat at a popular chain restaurant. I checked emails and the latest news on my phone while enduring a lengthy line. The man behind me had a troubling, repetitive cough and was standing far too close. I probably wouldn't have noticed if I hadn't been in a foul mood. But every time I took a step forward, he was right on my heels. I had simply had enough at this point and wanted my space. So, I did what any rational person would do. I stumbled backward and *accidentally* bumped into him. "Oops . . . excuse me," I implored in a nice, rational voice that concealed my rage.

Finally, it was my turn to order. By now, I was hungry and angry or what my kids call "hangry." So, of course, I overordered, selecting a chicken burrito bowl with virtually every option *and* a cheese quesadilla.

I paid and waited while they finished preparing my food. They called my name and handed me a bag without the quesadilla. I told the disinterested employee at the register. He shrugged and asked his colleague to make a cheese quesadilla.

I waited. At this point, no one wanted to stand too close. At least I had that going for me.

After receiving my full order, I walked halfway around the mall, back up the escalator, through the department store and into the parking garage. At the garage exit, there were automated pay stations. I inserted my parking ticket at one of the stations. The ticket was rejected.

I tried another station. The ticket was rejected, again. I pressed a button on the machine to call for assistance. No one answered.

I cursed out loud.

I found a worker outside of the department store and angrily explained my problem. As he tried to direct me to customer service on the second floor, I interrupted. "I know where it is." I then mumbled something about customer service being some sort of oxymoron.

I'm sure the customer service representative was pleased to see me again. She explained that she wasn't sure she could help with the parking payment but offered to do better. She said she could validate my ticket.

I gave her my ticket, and she inserted it into her own reader. To her surprise, her system couldn't read my ticket. She explained that she couldn't validate my parking because the system could not read my ticket. I once again explained that her store "*sucks*."

Screw it. I returned to my car with my unpaid ticket in hand. I drove to the nearest exit. No one was working at the exit, and again the machine wouldn't accept my ticket. I pressed another button to call for help. They told me to go to parking level one for assistance.

At this point, I completely lost it. I yelled at the attendant to open the "bleeping" gate. I got back out of my car and entered the unmanned both in search of the lever to release me from this prison. I tried to lift the gate forcibly. I tried to get a new ticket from the incoming lane but couldn't.

Rage consumed me more than I could ever before remember.

I returned to my car, backed out of the lane, and drove to parking level one as instructed. I parked in one of the exit lanes, and then another car pulled up behind me. I tried my ticket in the machine just for the heck of it. It didn't work. I left my car in the line and went to an attendant in a nearby booth. I gave the attendant my ticket and explained my plight.

The attendant asked when I'd entered the garage, charged me two dollars, opened the gate, and sent me on my way.

All that for two dollars? I nearly lost my mind.

I returned to my hotel room nearly two hours after I began this journey. I emptied the contents of my dinner bag on the desk. Of course, there was no fork or knife. I slammed my fists on the desk and exhorted my God, "*What else could possibly go wrong?*" I called room service and requested that they send a fork and knife to my room.

Then God answered my question.

I decided to get some ice for my water. After returning with ice in hand, I discovered my room key didn't work. Off I went to the front desk. The adventure continued.

I'm not proud of this story. As outrageous as it may seem, I assure you that I haven't exaggerated the details. Actually, the nature and duration of my reactions are understated.

I reacted to circumstances in ways that weren't helpful and made matters worse. I can rationalize all I want about the circumstances: I had work to do; I was tired from my trip; Nothing was going my way; The service I received wasn't good.

While all of these may be true, I have to ask myself, how did my reactions help or hinder me? Was there a better way for me to respond? What could I have done differently?

To this day, I believe that God was testing me. I was proud of the progress I'd been making as a person. I was proud of my intentional efforts to pursue healthy balance and restore my life priorities. However, I was still flawed. How much of my effort was genuine and sincere? I'm human.

While I can't guarantee that a more sane and calm response would've helped resolve the issues I faced, I can definitively say that my reactions didn't help in any way and the events colored my disposition far longer than they should have. I didn't sleep well as I relived each encounter. Because I was tired and less prepared, I wasn't at my best as a facilitator the next day. However, perhaps in his own mysterious way, God equipped me with new material about reactions in the workplace to discuss during my facilitated workshop.

Have you ever had a day like mine? Worse yet, do you frequently react in an undesirable way to circumstances that may or may not be within your control? What fuels your negative reactions? Is it fear? Is it shame? Is it worry? Is it comparison? In my case, a lack of patience has always been my greatest challenge.

Several years ago, my family gave me a Dammit Doll for Christmas. I opened the present in front of my wife, children, and extended family. They sheepishly laughed as I pulled it out of the box and read the inscription:

Whenever things don't go so well,
And you want to hit the wall and yell,
Here's a little dammit doll,
That you can't do without.
Just grasp it firmly by the legs
And find a place to slam it.
And as you whack the stuffing out,
Yell, "Dammit! Dammit! Dammit!"

Later, I thought more deeply about this little gag gift. I stopped seeing the humor. Rather, it was clear that my children saw me being angry . . . or as they say, "raging." I decided to do what I often do, observe and write.

I spent the next two weeks observing my reactions. I noted the people, places, things, or circumstances that caused me to react in a positive or negative manner. I noted the impact my reactions had on me physically and mentally. I decided not to judge my reactions. Rather, I just wrote them in my journal. Below are two of the more prominent entries:

- On my way home from work today, traffic was extra heavy. I could feel my chest tighten as tension grew in my body. I wanted desperately to be home. I was stressed and needed to decompress. I tried to change lanes on multiple occasions. It only made matters worse. I became more frustrated. Eventually, I came upon the accident that was holding up traffic. How dare I complain.

- I spent two hours this afternoon working on a proposal for work from my home office. I was on a roll and creating good content.

Then the "spinning wheel" appeared on my screen. MS Word locked up. I slammed the desk and cursed. The wheel remained. I mumbled aloud and punched the escape key multiple times. In my haste, I rebooted the computer only to discover that I'd lost approximately the last half hour of my work. I cursed again, only louder this time, and brashly left the office only to find both kids glancing timidly my way from the next room. What kind of example am I?

To my credit, there were several more positive reactions noted in my journal as well. In most such cases, I was interacting directly with other people. When my son spilled a cup of milk, I calmly explained that these things happen and helped to clean the mess. When a colleague at work made a mistake, I thanked him for acknowledging the mistake, shared a similar story of my own, and offered to help him rectify the error.

Following two weeks and sixteen journal entries, I examined my list for commonality. Two things immediately jumped out at me. First, I'm impatient with *things* that slow my progress. I'm efficient and driven to produce, and any things that slow my progress generate a negative reaction. Such circumstances occasionally cause me to raise my voice (yell), curse, or both—something I otherwise never do. Worse yet, my children see it and hear it.

The second observation is that I'm patient with people. Notwithstanding my reaction in the Crystal City Mall, I typically allow people much more grace and understanding. If people slow down my progress, I'm much more forgiving. If behaviors need to be corrected, I provide feedback in an empathetic manner.

While this second observation is good, I had to dig deeper into the rationale. I'm guessing that my calm reaction to people is tightly connected to my tendency to be a people-pleaser. Likewise, it may reflect my desire not to be judged as impatient. Am I simply better hiding my internal frustrations to present the image that I want you to have of me?

This latter question is worth digging deeper into in Chapter 13 on Integrity. Regardless of the answer to my question, I knew that I had to address my patience or lack thereof. I took intentional steps and had made considerable progress. However, as my story in the Crystal City Mall shows and my children will attest, I experience the occasional relapse. Now, instead of cursing the world for imposing upon me such awful circumstances, I thank God for not-so-subtle reminders to *CEEK a Better Way*.

I encourage you to consider the people, places, things, or circumstances that generate strong emotional reactions in you. Capture the circumstances and your thoughts in your journal. Assess the situations and search for commonality. Assess the underlying motivation or objective that drives the reaction. Don't judge that motivation, for it will tell you much about yourself. Prepare to dig deep into how such motivations and reactions affect your disposition. How you show up in the world will have a significant impact on your pursuit of healthy balance as it directly impacts your self-esteem, the health of your relationships, and personal fulfillment.

 ## Journal – Questions to Consider

- What people, places, things, or circumstances generate positive or negative reactions in me?
- What is the reason or underlying motivation for my reactions?
- How do such reactions help or hinder me?

 ## Exercise – Consider a Deeper Dive

Spend two weeks noting your reactions to people, places, things, or circumstances that generate strong emotions, positive and negative. Describe the circumstances in your journal, and write your rationale for your reaction. Don't judge your reactions. Simply acknowledge them and write down your observations.

Assess your disposition

The Dalai Lama has suggested that if you have a fear or anxiety, you should examine it. He offered two subsequent options based on your examination:

1. If there is something you can do about it, why worry?
2. If there is nothing you can do about it, why worry?

How much time, energy, and emotional capital do you exhaust by worrying? As I'm writing this part of the book, I dropped my fourteen-year-old son off at the Raleigh/Durham Airport at 5:50 a.m. It's a Friday morning, and he's traveling from North Carolina to Miami, Florida, with his soccer team for a couple of games over the weekend. He's already stressed from a long week of school and practices, and overwhelmed by the homework he must complete during his trip. He's anxious about games planned against the top programs from Florida. He's overtired and well-aware that he'll need to wake up early on Saturday as well as Sunday, which also happens to be the day we lose an hour to daylight savings time. His team is expected to return Sunday evening around 10:30 p.m., and he's not looking forward to getting up Monday at 6:15 a.m. to go to school and then soccer practice.

Am I happy about the circumstances of the trip? No. Is there anything I can do about it? Perhaps.

My son, with the support of my wife and me, accepted an invitation to play on the North Carolina Football Club (NCFC) Academy soccer team. We knew this would place significant demands on his time, but it's a passion for which he's shown great potential. There would be travel, some missed school, and associated stresses. But we had already weighed the pros and cons and supported our son in his pursuit of playing a high-level of soccer.

As I drove my son to the airport, I reflected on all we had done to prepare him for the trip and to ease his mind. We helped pack his bags. We enjoyed a peaceful dinner the night before as a family. I gave him a massage. My wife reviewed the agenda with him and provided assurance regarding logistics. We got him to bed early—well earlier than usual.

I considered the advice of the Dalai Lama. Was there anything else I could do to alleviate any fear or anxiety about the trip that my son and I had? I suggested to him that we say a prayer for a safe and success-ful trip. I prayed out loud that my son would be at peace. I asked God to look after him and to instill in his heart the comfort and knowledge that he's accepted and loved just the way he is.

I dropped my son off, gave him a big hug, and drove away. Why worry? I don't.

If you want healthy balance, do everything in your power to eliminate unnecessary worry. Take the initiative to address what you can regard-ing the things that you worry about and then stop worrying. For me, making my faith a priority in my life was the most significant factor in reducing my tendency to worry. I don't profess to have all the answers about God and faith, but I'm comfortable surrendering outcomes to a higher power, as well as random chance. What can you do to surrender outcomes? Prepare and let go.

Pessimists take worry to incredible heights. Merriam-Webster defines a pessimist as a person who habitually sees or anticipates the worst or is disposed to be gloomy. In contrast, an optimist is disposed to take a favorable view of events or conditions and to expect the most favorable outcome.

As you think about the reactions you have to people, places, things, or circumstances, it's important to assess the underlying motivation for your reaction, as well as the mood or disposition that's most closely associated with it. My lack of patience, for example, mani-fests in my desire to get things done without external events affect-ing my progress. The result is a mood or disposition that most would describe as angry or frustrated. Unfortunately, that mood would often color the next hour, the next day, or even the next week. As noted by Chalmers Brothers in his book *Language and the Pursuit of Happiness*:

> When we're in a mood, it's interesting to notice that we're usually not value-neutral about the mood. That is, instead we tend to be "champions" of our own mood, doing our best to enroll others in it with us. We become the poster child for whatever mood we're in, and we get very 'Right' about being in the mood. It becomes the Right mood to be in, and we justify it by saying things such as 'If you had happen to you what I had happen to me, you'd be in this mood, too!'

It's important to assess how our tendency to react affects our general disposition and vice versa.

Am I angry because I react? Or do I react because I am angry?

Do I worry because I jump to conclusions? Or do I jump to conclusions because I worry?

Do I fear because I'm afraid? Or am I afraid because I fear?

I think it's safe to say that both sides of each statement are generally true in each of the above examples. What I know from personal experience is that I often look for situations to validate my mood. I was quick to ignore the kindness of the customer service representative who tried to validate my ticket in Crystal City Mall. However, I wouldn't ignore the coughing man who stood too close to me in the line at the restaurant. I was impatient, frustrated, and angry. That man reinforced my perceived right to my current emotion. When I'm impatient, I look for circumstances to validate my impatience.

Psychologists refer to this as confirmation bias, or a tendency to search for or interpret information in a way that confirms one's preconceptions. In other words, if you're a Democrat, you look for and find validation of Democratic views, policies, and candidates. Likewise, if you're a Republican, you look for and find validation of Republican views, policies, and candidates. This tendency permeates all of our belief systems to include politics, religion, social concerns, and life in general.

Our tendency to confirm our beliefs also colors our views of organizations, individuals, and ourselves. If you deem an organization to be corrupt, you'll seek and advance situations that support your assumption. If you believe someone is arrogant, self-centered, or simply unkind, you'll look for signs to rationalize their self-orientation. If you feel that you're unattractive, treated unfairly, or unworthy, you will surely discover the evidence to promote your theory.

Fortunately, confirmation bias isn't a theory that only serves to reinforce a negative disposition. Research on the practice of expressing gratitude discovered confirmation bias works to affirm a positive disposition. If you focus daily time, attention, and thought to reflect on the blessings of your life, you'll surely be a happier person. And, if you believe you're fulfilled and happy, you'll be quick to discover the circumstances that reinforce this narrative.

In April 2012, Hans Villarica wrote an article in *The Atlantic* titled "How the Power of Positive Thinking Won Scientific Credibility." The article summarized an interview with psychologist Michael F. Scheier as he reflected on the impact of, and progress since, his 1985 research regarding the power of optimism. In that year, Dr. Scheier and his colleague Charles S. Carver published "Optimism, Coping, and Health: Assessment and Implications of Generalized Outcome Expectancies." Their research included a simple test of hopefulness and an optimism scale that has since served as an effective tool in bridging the gap between psychology and biology and measuring the impact and healing powers of positive psychology. Their work has been cited in more than three thousand published works since it was first introduced.

In the words of Dr. Scheier:

> I think it's now safe to say that optimism is clearly associated with better psychological health, as seen through lower levels of depressed mood, anxiety, and general distress,

when facing difficult life circumstances, including situations involving recovery from illness and disease. A smaller, but still substantial, amount of research has studied associations with physical well-being. And I think most researchers at this point would agree that optimism is connected to positive physical health outcomes, including decreases in the likelihood of re-hospitalization following surgery, the risk of developing heart disease, and mortality.

Through the work of Dr. Scheier, Dr. Carver, and others since, the term *dispositional optimism* has been defined as the general expectation that good things versus bad things will happen. It's a stable, trait-like personality characteristic comprised of a general, positive mood or attitude about the future and a tendency to anticipate a favorable outcome to life situations. In contrast, *dispositional pessimism* reflects a general, negative expectation for the future.

There's no doubt that my tendency toward pessimism contributed to a self-perpetuating lack of healthy balance and personal fulfillment. I was convinced that the world conspired against me. My boss was incentivized to squeeze every ounce of effort from my soul. My clients placed their challenges on my back so they could sleep well at night. My colleagues worked to leverage or undermine my efforts for personal gain. Even my family demanded constant attention to the neglect of my well-being.

Such pessimism can influence larger life views as well:

"The opposition party is out to get me and my money."

"My church condemns me and also seeks to get my money."

"The world is overcome by natural disasters, terrorist attacks, and inexplicable violence."

"Bad things happen to good people."

And how often do pessimistic tendencies steal joy from simple, everyday circumstances?

"Of course, it rained today . . . of all days."

"These drivers just want me to be late . . . yet again."

"If I get screwed at the drive-through window . . . one more time."

"My child is being mistreated; it happens every time."

"Life is unfair."

And most significant for me was how often pessimistic thoughts influenced my self-esteem. I was overworked. I was tired. I was unhealthy. I was judged. I didn't measure up. I was unhappy. I wasn't fulfilled. I was unworthy.

Imagine the impact, if these thoughts occupy the majority of the fifty, sixty, or seventy thousand thoughts you have on a daily basis. What would be the impact? Is it self-perpetuating? As confirmation bias implies, do you seek rational explanations to validate your disposition?

There is a debate about whether the general characteristics of optimism versus pessimism are inherited. Is it nature versus nurture? I suspect there's a little bit of both. While I'm not a scientist and can't definitively prove it one way or another, I am a human. I know firsthand that if you change your mind, you can change your life. A renewed perspective and positive disposition will promote healthy balance and personal fulfillment. It takes practice. It takes intentionality. Stay with me as we now "Take the CONN" in pursuit of a healthier, more positive mind-set.

 Journal – Questions to Consider

- How do the people, places, things, or circumstances that generate undesirable reactions color my general mood or disposition?
- How do these circumstances impact my tendency toward dispositional optimism or pessimism?
- How do such circumstances affect how I show up in the priority areas of my life?

Exercise – Consider a Deeper Dive

Return to the list of activities or routines you defined for the priority areas of your life. For each activity or routine, consider the impact that your general disposition has on your appreciation of the priority and the activity. Note these observations in your journal.

Take the CONN

At CEEK LLC, we intentionally defined our culture to serve as a differentiator to the people we hire, the clients we serve and the communities we support. As part of our *Intentional Culture Plan*, we described a set of behaviors and rituals that represent the tangible application of our core values. One of those behavior statements is, *"Believe it before you see it."*

This statement is intended to reinforce the creativity and problem-solving nature of the CEEK team. We recognize and acknowledge the power of positive thinking. We challenge the status quo to *CEEK a Better Way*. We aren't constrained by the need to see something before we accept a new possibility. We create with the words we use and the thoughts we have. We aspire to a better way. We believe.

Complementary to this notion is a second behavior statement, *"Take the CONN,"* a common terminology used to assume ownership in controlling the movement of a ship. We *"take the CONN"* to assume ownership for the direction of our lives. We refuse to be victims of circumstances in professional and personal matters. We accept adversity and conflict for what they are. We take the initiative to address undesirable circumstances where we can and to accept what we can't change. We're solution-oriented. We're accountable. We steer the ship and assume responsibility to *CEEK a Better Way*.

If we *"believe it before we see it"* and we *"take the CONN"* to make it happen, virtually anything is possible. Working in concert, the application of these two behavior statements in your personal and professional life can have a dramatic effect on your disposition and pursuit of healthy life balance. When you think of your life circumstances, what do you believe? Are you blessed or are you cursed? Both can be rationalized and defended. What will you choose to believe? Believe it, and you will see it.

Furthermore, are you in control of your life and your general disposition? Or have you surrendered control to your boss, the client, your colleagues, your spouse or your significant other, or friends who may assess you and your "performance?" Are you steering the ship or along for the ride? Are you in the game, or are you a spectator? *"Take the CONN"* and choose your disposition.

With the exception of those dealing with anxiety, depression, or some other very real and debilitating mental illness, most of us have the potential to choose our disposition. We can *"take the CONN"* relative to our emotional state and how we show up in the world. We can choose to accept our circumstances as they are and be grateful for what we have. We can choose to be calm or reactive. We can choose to be satisfied or in need. We can choose to be an optimist or a pessimist.

This book has offered some helpful tips to discover healthy balance. Pursue a values-based mission. Define priorities and establish routines that reinforce those priorities. Be mentally present to such routines. While great advice, what good is any of it if you have a negative disposition? It's tough to make the case that you are living a healthy, balanced life if you show up as the despondent Eeyore to the priorities of your life.

I get it. Right now, you may be pushing back. That sounds nice in theory, but if you only knew my circumstances. My life is hard. I lost my job. My mother, father, spouse, or child is ill. I'm ill. My job is demanding and stressful. Or, it simply isn't my personality.

I'm not suggesting that you have to transform from the morose Eeyore to the bouncing Tigger. Nobody likes a phony Pollyanna. Whatever your circumstances, there must be steps you can take in a positive direction. I know it can be done. I took those steps. Over time, they build on each other. As you become intentional in your efforts to react differently, express gratitude, and choose a positive outlook, the mental exercise becomes self-perpetuating. Confirmation bias will kick in.

As I confessed earlier, I am impatient with things that slow my progress. I shared reactions that my children had seen when I faced technical problems in particular. Heck, they even gave me a Dammit Doll to help.

Several years ago, I conducted an experiment. Every time the "spinning wheel" showed up on my screen, which typically resulted in an abrupt shut down of my computer and lost work, I could choose a different response than my standard choice words followed by a lingering sour disposition.

The next time it happened, I decided to get up from my desk and find the nearest person to hug. My wife was pleasantly surprised. And after the kids caught on to the game, it turned into an unanticipated chase throughout the house. "Oh no! Here comes Pappa! Run for your life!" Eventually, I caught them and overcame the laughter enough to give them some form of a resisted embrace.

Not surprisingly, I'd return to my computer in a better mood. Sometimes the spinning wheel had disappeared, and I could return to my work. Sometimes it didn't. Either way, I had chosen an alternative reaction to undesirable behavior, and it worked. Though the stimulus was the same, the conscious response was different.

Unfortunately, computer issues or other things that slowed my progress weren't limited to my home office. I didn't think my boss or colleagues would appreciate me chasing them through the office for a hug when a technology problem reared its ugly head in the corporate setting.

So, there I was in the office in the middle of a critical project deadline. The computer froze, and the spinning wheel returned. I fought the urge to curse if only to protect my image (we'll get to such shallow motivations in Chapter 13). I thought about my new response at home. Instead of reacting in constrained anger, I remembered the *ball* that I now carry with me. I remembered that I'm not defined by what I produce, but rather the person I am.

I chose to pray.

I closed my eyes, said an "Our Father," and asked God to calm my nerves. I prayed for peace. I begrudgingly thanked God for adversity as a reminder that I'm human. I asked God to help me finish my work, so I could return home to my family. I opened my eyes; the spinning wheel was gone. I continued my work.

To this day, I have never been very disciplined with respect to prayer. As a family, we pray before meals, and I say a prayer with my kids at night. Otherwise, I sporadically pick times to ask God for things, often with selfish motivations. To be honest, I've always been somewhat suspect of so-called prayer warriors. Just squint your eyes hard. Listen more intently. Have a conversation. Really?

I can't say whether there was some sort of divine intervention that helped the first time I prayed at work. I'm guessing God may have more important matters to tend to. However, the simple act did calm my spirit and significantly changed my perspective and disposition. And, perhaps, that's the answer to the prayer. Perhaps that's a mini-miracle in itself.

I have since replaced chasing my kids through the house with a brief prayer and reflection when I face anything that slows my progress and tests my patience. Without a doubt, this ritual has enabled me to build a new habit and sustain a more favorable, positive disposition.

Like any recovering addict, I'd be remiss not to mention the occasional relapse. My kids may laugh as they read this, knowing that I recently raged while spending more than three hours over two days on the phone with our insurance company to secure a pre-authorization for a medical procedure for my daughter. Happily, I'm confident that my reactive incidents are far less frequent, and when they do happen, they are almost always followed by an unconditional apology.

My pursuit of healthy balance has only been enhanced by a more positive and optimistic disposition. Not only am I more present to the priorities in my life, but I choose to be present in a positive and inspirational, yet realistic, manner.

During the writing of this book, we were in the midst of a difficult three months. My sixteen-year-old daughter, an aspiring college gymnast, injured her knee, requiring surgery and a six-month recovery. Are her dreams shot? My son, an aspiring college soccer player, had an emergency room visit to investigate a recurring and sustained, elevated heart rate after practice. What impact will this have on his life? My wife, a former athlete who aspires to stay in the game, recently injured her knee and shoulder. Are running and exercise no longer possibilities? And not to be outdone, our dog Moxie, requires surgery to repair a torn ACL—her second. Will she experience the joy of running free again?

I wouldn't wish these circumstances on anyone much less those closest to me. Any member of my family, myself included, could choose to dwell on the negative. We certainly allow the space to be upset, to express grief, and to cry as needed. In my daughter's case, this was her second major surgery before her seventeenth birthday. She was understandably mad at God. Her junior season was lost, and the college coaches stopped calling. Life wasn't fair.

The good news is, she's going to be just fine. The time off from the gym enabled her to focus on her academic studies during the notorious junior-year rigor. She had a much-needed opportunity to rest her body. She also showed great emotional strength and friendship in support of her teammates, who were doing the one thing she desperately wanted to do. After her recovery, my daughter restored her strength and began working hard to return to the gym stronger than ever. Don't bet against my daughter! And, regardless of a future gymnastics career or not, she's well-prepared for life. What more could a parent ask for?

I choose to accept what I can't change. And I choose to bring a positive solution-oriented mind-set when faced with adverse situations. We have a saying in our family: "Leverage adversity as an opportunity to teach." That's what adversity is and should be. My hope and prayer are that our children are learning the value of these lessons far sooner than I did. For the record, my daughter has since accepted an offer to compete in college, my son is back on the fields without skipping a beat, my wife has resumed her exercise routine, and Moxie is once again unstoppable.

Don't spend your life trying to avoid adversity because you can't. Instead, build awareness of how you respond to it. Intentionally design a more desirable response. Practice this new response and establish a new habit. Give yourself the freedom to fail. Bad habits take time to break, and new habits take time to form. In fact, according to research on habits first suggested by Noel Burch of Gordon Training International, most of us will go through the following four stages in our pursuit of new, healthy habits:

1. Unconscious and Incompetent: I'm not even aware of a habit and its negative impact on me, my disposition, and others.
2. Conscious and Incompetent: I'm now aware of a negative habit and its impact, but I continue to exhibit behaviors consistent with the habit.
3. Conscious and Competent: I'm aware of a negative habit and able to choose an alternative response as I consciously consider the circumstances.
4. Unconscious and Competent: I'm unaware of the old habit and simply respond in a more positive way without having to consider the circumstances.

Hopefully, you're now conscious of negative habits, responses, emotions, etc., that you exhibit in response to adversity or certain people, places, things, or circumstances. It's now time to plan an alternative response and form a new habit. Where and how do you start?

A place to start may be Will Bowen's "Complaint Free" challenge. In 2006, Pastor Bowen served as the minister of a small Midwestern church. As he delivered a series of sermons on prosperity, he noticed his congregants, while claiming they wanted prosperity, were busy complaining about what they already had. Seeing the disconnect, he challenged his congregation to go twenty-one days without complaining, a timeframe typically associated with creating a new habit. He gave a purple rubber bracelet to everyone in attendance and instructed them to switch the bracelet to the other wrist each time they found themselves complaining. The caveat was that each time they switched the bracelet, the twenty-one-day clock started again. Participants would continue the challenge until they reached twenty-one consecutive days without a complaint.

Pastor Bowen's "Complaint Free World" project exploded from 250 bracelets to a movement of more than eleven million people worldwide. As evidenced by the daily letters he receives, the Complaint Free challenge improved the lives of millions of people, who have built an awareness of their thoughts and reactions and consciously chose an alternative approach.

This example illustrates what it means to *"take the CONN."* What will be your twenty-one-day challenge? What negative thoughts and emotions are you going to address? Will it be fear, anger, worry, or impatience? Is it simply a negative attitude? Choose dispositional optimism. Believe it before you see it. Build a new habit. Establish a new bias toward positivity and observe how the world confirms your bias.

Journal – Questions to Consider

- How do I generally show up in the world? How would I like to show up in the world?
- Using your list of people, places, things or circumstances that generate negative reactions, ask: What is a better, alternative reaction to such circumstances?
- What can I do to build a new habit in how I respond?

Exercise – Consider a Deeper Dive

Select three of the most common circumstances that cause an undesired reaction. For each, plan an alternative response. Practice the response for three weeks and note the impact on your general mood and disposition, as well as the impact on your participation in the activities and routines that reinforce the priorities in your life. Record your thoughts in your journal, including any perceived impact on your productivity, balance, relationships, and general fulfillment.

CHAPTER 12

PLAY

We don't stop playing because we grow old;
we grow old because we stop playing.

~ George Bernard Shaw

Close the book. Embrace your inner child. Play.

CHAPTER 13

EMBRACE A BROADER INTEGRITY

The Chinese define image in these terms: there are three mirrors that form a person's reflection; the first is how you see yourself, the second is how others see you and the third mirror reflects the truth. Know yourself, know the truth.

~ Robin Sharma

You're now inspired by a values-based purpose. You're present to renewed priorities and the associated rituals. And you're working toward a more positive, optimistic outlook. Yes indeed, you are well on your way to discovering healthy life balance.

But if you lack integrity, none of this will matter. When was the last time you heard any of the following?

"I cheated on my timecard and taxes this year, which gave me more free time and extra spending money. I feel much more fulfilled."

"By simply neglecting half the commitments I made at work and at home, I was able to restore a strong sense of healthy balance."

"Well, I would never behave that way at church or at home, but I found it enhances my value in my organization and the image my friends have of me. It helps me attain a higher level of peace and fulfillment."

Many organizations and individuals claim *integrity* as one of their core values. When I ask them what that means, the typical response is that they don't lie, cheat, or steal. They follow the rules and maintain high standards of honesty and ethics. While this is all good and appropriate, this response only reflects one of three critical components of integrity. At CEEK, we refer to these components as the three "W's" of integrity. This chapter will give you valuable insights and a broader definition of integrity that will help you:

- Honor your worth
- Honor your word
- Honor your wholeness

Living an authentic life of integrity is the final key to your discovery of healthy life balance.

Honor your worth

In the book, *Missoula,* by Jon Krakauer, the author tells an old story. It's about a lawyer who, after winning a client's big case, cables the client with the following message: "Justice has prevailed." Upon receiving the message, the client fires off a return telegram: "Appeal immediately."

The client confirms that victory, not justice, was the objective. We've all heard the phrase, "win at all costs." Really? Are we willing to sacrifice justice in pursuit of victory? Does the end justify the means? Will you promote healthy balance by sacrificing your morality, values, and integrity for personal gain?

"Honor your worth" refers to the most common definition of integrity. It represents adherence to moral and ethical principles. It's often described as doing the right thing when no one is watching. Guess what? Someone is always watching.

If you lack this form of integrity, you diminish your worth. You devalue yourself. And unless you truly lack the internal sense of decency and the ability to inherently distinguish right from wrong, a lapse of this form of integrity will weigh on you for months, years, and even a lifetime. Healthy balance is not attainable under such weight.

In the extreme, a lapse of this form of integrity is difficult to overcome. If you cheated on a spouse, stole from your employer, used performance-enhancing drugs, lied on a resume, committed a crime; or harmed another for personal gain, the stigma and guilt will linger. Likely, you'll attempt to conceal your indiscretion, willing it away and never realizing that the best long-term solution is to bring it to light. The sooner, the better. As the saying goes, the cover-up is worse than the crime.

How many stories do we need to hear of the politician, the business-man or woman, the famous musician, the Hollywood producer, or the athlete who succumbed to the allure of riches, fame, and power? How we love to judge the rich and the famous! Maybe you even experience pleasure when those who represent different views, play for enemy teams, or simply have what you desire fall from grace. Most of us state, often with an air of condemnation, that we'd never fall prey to such unethical, malicious, or dishonest behavior.

While I'd like to think that I'd never take performance enhancing drugs, I was never on the cusp of a professional career while working to overcome a career-threatening injury. And, while I've always been faithful to my wife, I've never been pursued relentlessly by beautiful women everywhere I go. Finally, while I'm proud of my track record in business ethics, I haven't faced make or break business decisions that could have dramatically changed my financial situation.

The reality is that most of the significant ethical lapses we hear of in the media or elsewhere aren't solely the result of a single decision. Rather, they occur when opportunity meets preparation. While the opportunity may represent a singular event that presents itself to any human being at any time, preparation is the progressive pushing of boundaries that makes one more leap possible. In other words, if you push the boundaries of ethical and moral behavior over time, you'll modify what you believe to be appropriate or acceptable behavior. Worse yet, your new threshold becomes reasonable behavior, which you think you can conceal.

The doping culture that invaded the world of professional cycling is a perfect example. We all know the story of Lance Armstrong and his defiant fall from grace. Perhaps the story of a lesser known cyclist is a more applicable example for most of us. In 1990, at the age of fifteen, Joe Papp was a cycling enthusiast. He sent a letter to the federation for professional cycling, USA Cycling, asking about his prospects as a professional cyclist and opportunities to compete in the sport. He'd found his passion and was encouraged by USA Cycling's response.

In 1994, Joe joined the U.S. national team and experienced early success. Eventually, he went to college and graduated from the University of Pittsburgh. All was well in the life of a great student and athlete. Then he returned to cycling.

Joe quickly discovered that guys he used to beat had passed him by, literally and figuratively. Those known as sprinters were now advanced climbers and vice versa. In some cases, he felt like his fellow competitors were passing him on mountain climbs as though they were on motorcycles. Joe was dismayed and depressed.

It was at this point that a teammate from New Zealand introduced him to a local doctor. This doctor prescribed a drug called erythropoietin. More commonly known as EPO, erythropoietin is a peptide hormone produced naturally in the body to stimulate red blood cell production. EPO increases oxygen absorption, reduces fatigue and enhances healing, but it comes with a host of dangerous potential side effects.

Because Joe obtained his prescription for EPO from a certified medical doctor, he rationalized his first use for legitimate medical reasons. Because the drug seemed to be working, Joe continued taking EPO and soon caught and even passed his colleagues.

Eventually, there was a shortage of EPO in the U.S. Another friend introduced Joe to a production source in China. Now Joe's boundaries of what was legitimate and acceptable had begun to expand. Most everyone was doing it, and using EPO was the only "legitimate" way to compete. He contacted the producer and secured a steady source for the foreseeable future.

After some fellow riders expressed dismay at the lack of reliable U.S. sources, Joe rationalized that he could "help" his friends. Rather than connecting them to his source, he'd just order on their behalf. Eventually, his clientele grew beyond a select group of friends to anonymous requestors.

Joe was now a certified drug dealer.

How does someone go from being a good student, an exceptional athlete, and an outstanding member of their community one day to an imprisoned drug dealer the next? What husband or wife transitions from a loving and doting spouse one day to an adulterer the next? What politician runs their first campaign by saying, "I can be bought!" as their platform? These things never happen in the moment. Somewhere, somehow the person began to push and rationalize the boundaries of acceptable or ethical behavior. It's always a series of progressive decisions within the context of an ever-expanding boundary of "appropriate" behaviors.

I'd like to believe that no one interviews for a job saying, "I see that immoral and unethical behavior is one of your core values. That aligns well with my career aspirations. I think you'll find I bring a wealth of relevant qualifications and experience." With the possible exception of significant mental illness, I don't believe anyone grows up seeking to cheat the system to get ahead. Universities don't offer advanced degrees in "bribery, extortion, and embezzlement."

Joe Papp certainly had no intention or expectation of becoming a convicted drug dealer. His passion combined with opportunity led him down an unintended yet dishonorable path. He failed to set appropriate boundaries along the way with each progressive step seeming to be more reasonably justified. (To his credit, Joe Papp accepted responsibility for his mistakes and is now a strong, anti-doping advocate who shares his personal story openly to help others.)

In spite of our good intentions, unethical behavior is far too prevalent. Why? Because when little transgressions go unchecked, they build on each other. Little transgressions evolve into big transgressions. Then we're trapped. We become a servant to our image or lifestyle. The economic, mental, and physical cost of coming clean is simply unbearable. And we flat out ignore the spiritual impact—our shame won't allow it.

Is it worth it? Is healthy balance attainable under these circumstances? The answer is a resounding No!

The key to "honoring your worth" and sustaining this form of integrity is to put in place the appropriate guardrails that will confront and prevent the small lapses that might lead to bigger lapses. Just like the guardrails on a road aren't located in the most dangerous part of the road, so too are the guardrails in your life. They should be placed in a safe space that's approaching dangerous territory.

The following list represents a few simple examples of the guardrails I apply in my personal and professional life. Adherence to them ensures that I remove the potential for seemingly innocent lapses of judgment that could lead to more significant lapses of honesty and ethics.

- *Never travel alone with an individual of the opposite sex:* While I'd like to think that this is an unnecessary guardrail, that's the point. Why put yourself or another party in a situation that could lead to something inappropriate or that could be misconstrued?

- *Return all pain medication after the immediate need:* In case you haven't been paying attention, there's an opioid epidemic in our nation. Between my daughter, wife, and me, we've endured six surgeries over the last seven years. Why would I even allow the temptation to exist? We return unused medications to the pharmacy.

- *One may drink, but never both:* When we drive to a meal or event, my wife *or* I may order one or two drinks. We ensure that the driver doesn't drink alcohol. Why would we ever put ourselves in a situation that could adversely affect our lives, or that of others, for a couple drinks? This rule has the added benefit of demonstrating responsibility to our kids. I occasionally hand the keys to my wife in front of our children after stating out loud, "I'd like to order a beer tonight. Will you drive home?"

- *Let my gut speak:* When it comes to ethical dilemmas, we often say listen to our gut. I practice the habit of letting my gut speak.

If I'm ever in a business setting where I feel squeamish, I let others know that I feel squeamish. I not only listen to my gut, but I give it a voice. It's amazing how quickly a group responds if and when the potential for something unethical is verbalized. To be clear, the voice of my gut doesn't judge or accuse. It's a guardrail that, selfishly-speaking, helps prevent me from going along with anything questionable.

I can provide dozens of examples in my professional career where this last point has played out. Several years ago, I was asked to change hours on my timecard to align to contract renewal dates and funding. My gut said no. I was once instructed to inform staff that a senior leader chose to leave the company on his own accord after we had earlier seen him escorted from the building. My gut spoke clearly. I once watched as an executive demeaned and belittled a businesswoman by suggesting that if he wore a skirt, he might be able to get a meeting with a target client, too. My gut cried foul! In each situation, I listened to my gut and spoke up.

Could I have let these transgressions go? Perhaps. Did my response hinder me professionally? Who cares? Did my intentional effort to speak from my gut prevent me from heading down a slippery slope of questionable behavior? Who knows?

And that's the point. Why put yourself in a potential position to head down a slippery slope? I assure you, I never say, "If only I hadn't put that silly guardrail in place. I could have had so much more." Rather, I'm grateful for the guardrails in my life. I credit these guardrails as a contributing factor in my pursuit and discovery of healthy life balance.

 Journal – Questions to Consider

- How have small lapses of judgment led to bigger transgressions in my life?
- Where in my life might my honesty and ethics be tested?
- What guardrails can I adopt to honor my worth?

Exercise – Consider a Deeper Dive

Identify three instances from your experience and relationships where people were exposed for unethical behavior. What circumstances led to these behaviors? (If you don't know, imagine what circumstances may have led to them.) Identify a point at which the individual could have or should have drawn the line or put a stop to the sequence of events that led to the unethical behavior. Identify and commit to three guardrails that will protect you from a series of events that could lead to similar circumstances. Apply these guardrails and note the impact.

Honor your word

Recently, I had a coaching client tell me about a request her boss had made to her on a Monday morning. The request went something like this.

"I know that you have been very busy, but if you can find the time and it's not too much trouble, could you draft a status report for the project?"

"Sure," she responded. And that was that.

One week later, her boss returned and asked, "Have you completed the status report?"

"No," she said with some surprise. "I've had other priorities."

"Well, I need that report for tomorrow's update to the leadership team," her boss responded.

Who's at fault? Logically, you can make the argument that the employee implied that she would complete the report. On the other hand, her boss made a conditional request without any specifics. Her boss surrendered not just the determination of "when" she would do the work, but also the priority or "if" she would do the work.

The second form of integrity is represented by honoring your word. In other words, you follow through on your commitments. When you say you will do something, you do it. People trust that it will get done. You show up on time. You're responsive. You follow through.

Unfortunately, we'll all fail at times relative to this form of integrity. Many of us make well-intentioned commitments that may be unfulfilled or unattainable because of unexpected events. Unlike ethical lapses associated with honoring your worth, it's much easier to restore this form of integrity. If we fail to honor our word, we can acknowledge the mistake and pursue a corrective course of action. That being said, it's important to your personal and professional reputation to establish yourself as someone who honors your word. More important, it's critical to your healthy pursuit of balance to establish the discipline to effectively manage your commitments so that you can maintain your integrity and honor your word.

The most common reasons for failing to honor our word are unclear agreements and a tendency to overcommit. The scenario I described above with a coaching client is a perfect example of the first reason. The request was vague. So was the response. The result is an unclear agreement at best. If you ask *who's at fault*, the answer is a resounding BOTH.

In his book, *Language and the Pursuit of Happiness*, Chalmers Brothers details the six elements of an effective request as follows:

1. A Committed Speaker
2. A Committed Listener
3. Future Action and Conditions of Satisfaction
4. Timeframe
5. Mood
6. Context

Items three, four, and six generally represent the content or substance of the request itself. The future actions and conditions of satisfaction detail the nature of the request. In other words, what's being asked, and what criteria determine successful fulfillment of the request. Timeframe refers to a deadline or when the action needs to be acted upon or completed. Context provides the rationale, as in what's the reason and ultimate value of the request being made?

Examining my client's dilemma, we will find that the request made was lacking in all three areas. Her boss provided no specifics relative to what should be in the status report, the length, format, etc. Clearly, the boss didn't indicate the timeframe or even allude to any sense of urgency. Lastly, the boss made no reference to the reason for the request. In many cases, explaining the purpose of the request provides further clarity around what should be done and offers additional motivation to complete it.

Once I pointed out the omissions from her boss' request, my client felt validated. She basked temporarily in the comfort of being *right*.

Unfortunately, her good feelings didn't last. I asked her what she should have done differently, and our conversation continued for another fifteen minutes.

How often are you complicit in perpetuating ineffective requests and thus vague, or what Brothers refers to as "criminal" agreements? Do you ever respond positively to a request knowing full well that you have no intention of fulfilling it? Or, more commonly, do you respond positively to a request accepting that the vagueness of the request gives you the leverage you need to interpret the terms and conditions of the request in a favorable manner?

Recently, my wife called while I was coming home one evening from a client site. She was running the kids to their usual afterschool activities. She had one simple request: "Can you make dinner tonight?"

"Sure," I said. "No problem."

While I like to think that I'm more than capable of cooking a variety of meals, my kids will tell you differently. When Pappa cooks, they predict with 99 percent accuracy that we'll have tacos. As I finished the call with my wife, I'd already mentally committed to the usual taco dinner that evening. For good measure, I considered also throwing in a salad.

To my dismay, I returned home to discover we didn't have the usual taco kit in the pantry, and we were out of hamburger meat. I took some chicken out of the freezer.

I decided to place the frozen chicken in a bowl of warm water to defrost it. I didn't want to repeat a past mistake of defrosting chicken in the microwave, which made it feel and taste like rubber. My plan was to let it thaw for an hour or so before throwing it on the grill. My daughter would probably be home around 7:00 p.m., but my son's practice always ran late. He and my wife wouldn't be home until well after 8:00 p.m. It would be a late dinner.

Since it was only 6:30 p.m., I turned on the TV and settled into the couch to relax for a half hour while the chicken slowly thawed in the bowl of lukewarm water. Just then the garage door opened. My daughter came into the house first. "What's for dinner?" she asked. My son followed. "I'm starving," he said. And then my perplexed wife entered. "Did you make dinner yet?" I mumbled some nonsense, consumed by the optics of my lazy butt sitting on the couch.

I could rationalize the misunderstanding all I want. I could even try to blame my wife for an "ineffective request." The bottom line is that I forgot the day of the week. The kids' practice schedules on Thursday are different than on Monday, Tuesday, and Wednesday. I also never clarified the conditions of the request (what to make) or timing (when to have dinner ready).

I had let my family down. They were tired, hungry, and disappointed. I did what any loving father and husband would do. I ran to the local Chick-fil-A in my best effort to make things right.

While this is a simple example, the real question is how pervasive your tendency is to live in a world of unclear requests and shallow or even criminal agreements? Worse yet, do you leverage the vague nature of the agreement to blame the other party for unmet expectations?

I've seen this tendency destroy the sanity within families. I've observed these behaviors destroy the culture of well-intentioned organizations. Practicing these bad habits isn't restricted to a limited set of small requests. If not recognized and addressed, the approach becomes the status quo for the majority of requests and associated agreements within families and organizations. The result is limited accountability and increased anxiety and stress. These aren't conditions conducive to healthy life balance, let alone successful organizations.

"Take the CONN." Take initiative. Whether you're the requestor or the recipient of a request, assume responsibility. Clarify the terms,

timeframe, and context. Ask the recipient of the request the questions necessary to gain clarity.

- What would you like to see in the status report?
- When do you need it by?
- What is the purpose?
- What would you like for dinner?
- What time would you like to eat?

Once you have effectively established the terms and conditions of a request, you're better prepared to determine the appropriate response. This leads us to the second most common reason that we fail to honor our word: a tendency to overcommit.

As I've admitted, I'm a recovering people-pleaser. By my nature, my default response to any request is yes. This tendency has led me down a slippery slope on many occasions, including contributing to me leading my son down a "slippery" driveway in an unmanned vehicle. This tendency led me down a slippery slope in my life.

In his book *Language and the Pursuit of Happiness,* Brothers continues to define four valid responses to an effective request. They are as follows:

1. Yes
2. No
3. Commit to commit
4. Counteroffer

I previously lived my life as though the first two responses were the only options. My default response was yes, and it pained me to say no. People trusted me and valued my support. I didn't want to let them down.

I started my rehab by adopting a new default response. For twenty-one days, I decided I would respond to any request, big or small, with a commitment to commit.

"Steve, would you like to go to lunch today?" "Let me get back to you in five minutes."

"Steve, can you pick up the kids from practice tonight?" "I'll check my schedule and let you know within the hour."

"Steve, can you volunteer this Friday evening at the church event?" "I'll discuss with my family and confirm with you tomorrow morning."

"Steve, can you manage this proposal effort for the team? It is due in two weeks." "Let me see if I can rearrange my other work and family commitments for the next two weeks. I will let you know within twenty-four hours."

"Steve, we would like to offer you a new job as the Director of Environmental Accounts!" "Let me think about my options and discuss them with my family and mentors. I'll let you know by 5:00 p.m. on Friday."

Big or small, I practiced for three weeks *not* making an immediate commitment to requests. It was hard. However, I discovered that I was much more inclined to say no after I had the opportunity to assess the request more thoroughly in light of other commitments and priorities, which brings us full circle to earlier exercises suggested in this book.

Having defined a values-driven mission and the priorities of my life, I'm better prepared to make decisions relative to the requests I receive. I use that mission, my stated priorities (and associated routines), and any identified slack as a filter for these decisions. If a request didn't reinforce my values and priorities, or if I did not have sufficient slack in my schedule, I said no to the request.

Now, you may be thinking, "This is nice in theory. But I work for a boss who doesn't accept no for an answer. I don't have the same flexibility in my professional life that I may have in my personal life."

I get it.

Like anything else, your response to a supervisor warrants some balance. In cases where requests are presented as nicely packaged demands, you can consider the option of a counteroffer. "I'm happy to fulfill your request but could use your help in determining what to take off my plate for the next week to ensure I have sufficient time to complete this new request."

While I can't address every possible scenario in this book, the point is to recognize the options available in response to requests and take ownership in more effectively managing the commitments you make. Don't be a victim of what you may see as the unreasonable demands of others. As Brothers states, "Learning how to say no can serve us. It is a powerful tool to enable us to manage our commitments. Without it, managing commitments is virtually impossible, and we very quickly realize that others are running our lives."

Once you improve your ability to manage your commitments, it's important to continue living and acting in a way that demonstrates you're someone who follows through on your commitments. You will be both trusted and trustworthy.

By being more intentional in my assessment of requests, I've restored some semblance of peace in my life. I now accept that a no response is not a rejection of the requestor. Rather, it's a rejection of the offer and a reflection of the value I place on the priorities in my life.

One simple example of how this plays out is in my response to the unending requests for various charitable contributions. For years, my wife and I would answer these calls and extend the courtesy of listening to their messages. While we would typically empathize with their cause, our decision to contribute was driven by an inability to say no. As a result, we'd donate twenty, fifty, or one hundred dollars here, there, and everywhere. We had no focus or filter within which to donate money and, more importantly, time. While giving money to well-intentioned charities isn't a bad thing, this tendency to agree and contribute with no real strategy or filter was an apt metaphor for virtually all aspects of my life.

Since defining our family values and a personal mission, we've decided to embrace Make-A-Wish and youth ministry at our church as our primary targets for giving. In doing so, we established a clearer picture of what we say no to and where we say yes. We've decided on a strategy to focus more time and resources in a smaller area rather than less time and resources to more organizations across a bigger pool. As a result, we've simplified our lives, are more inspired by what we do, and can meet our commitments consistently and honor our word. By extension, we no longer have to be everything to everyone.

Unfortunately, our culture and our tendency to compare drive us in the opposite direction. We are told or believe that we'll miss out by not committing to the next activity, the new assignment, or the latest compelling cause or trend. In turn, we're raising a generation of children who aren't well-equipped to manage commitments.

I marvel at the pressure placed on our kids. It's no longer enough to get decent grades and demonstrate a healthy balance of extracurricular activities to get into a good college. Youth coaches are encouraging specialization and extra training when a six-year-old displays the slightest proficiency in kicking a ball, shooting a basket, or catching a pass. If your fourth grader isn't in advanced math, they're doomed to failure. If your teenager hasn't accrued one hundred hours of demonstrated charitable activity, they risk losing their status in the National Honor Society, thereby hurting their college applications. What is the impact of this pressure? What message does it send?

Kids overcommit. Parents overcommit their kids. You and I are overwhelmed. Our children are stressed. Maybe this societal pressure will increase future demand for this book. I hope not.

When my son was ten years old, his soccer coaches saw what I already knew as my son's basketball coach. He has a special combination of an advanced sports IQ and athletic potential. At the time, he played on some so-called higher-level team. I had no idea what they called the various tiers and never really cared. After his fall season, the coach suggested that my son and his teammates participate on an indoor soccer team through the winter. He encouraged weekly pick-up futsal (a variant of soccer) games. He endorsed and handed out flyers for individualized athletic training sessions.

Seriously? They were ten. While all the parents talked and stressed about which activities to engage their children in, we took a novel approach. We asked our son. Instead of extending soccer through the winter, my son enjoyed a fun season of recreational basketball and simple, creative playtime with friends in the neighborhood. He later rejoined his burnt-out soccer friends for the spring season and picked up right where he'd left off.

As a competitive gymnast, our daughter spends twenty or more hours a week in the gym. Heading into her sophomore year of high school, she debated the number of advanced placement (AP) courses she should take. She felt the pressure. Friends were considering three to four AP courses. We value our daughter's mental and spiritual well-being more than her academic rigor. She took one AP course and a heavy dose of honors classes. She managed the workload well and added more AP courses her junior year. The demand on her time was significant but bearable. She'll take a slightly lighter workload her senior year. She found her sweet spot balancing her mental health with her drive to succeed.

Unfortunately, in my work with other high school students, I far too often have seen the impact of unreasonable pressure to excel. They schedule four, five, or even six AP courses a year. They volunteer through numerous venues to check a box on community service. They push themselves in a single, year-round sport to please someone else's expectations, never truly experiencing the joy of other available options. They endure countless hours of music instruction and practice to achieve the ever-elusive first chair in the band, part in the play, or applause from an unknown audience. Instead of getting the recommended eight to ten hours of sleep each night, they struggle to find six hours of rest.

When will we wake up? The alarm clock is ringing. Our children and we can no longer sustain the endless pressure of unclear and conflicting expectations. Bigger is not always better. Is it possible that less is more?

Manage your commitments. Leverage your values, purpose, and priorities as a filter to make decisions regarding what you will or won't do. Don't surrender control of your peace, fulfillment, and healthy balance to the expectations of others or, worse yet, our culture. Be a shining example of what it means to both give and receive clear requests. Honor your word.

 ### Journal – Questions to Consider

- How clear are the requests that I receive and make?
- Where in my life do I overcommit? What are the reasons that I make such commitments?
- What filters and behaviors can I adopt to better honor my word?

 ### Exercise – Consider a Deeper Dive

Identify three instances where you failed to follow through on a commitment. Assess the circumstances that contributed to both making the commitment and not following through. Were the request and eventual commitment clear? Identify what you would have done differently in retrospect. Document and practice three controls you can put in place to avoid making unreasonable commitments. Also, consider how you can better respond if and when you do miss a commitment. Practice these controls and note the impact.

Honor your wholeness

The term integrity is derived from the word integer: a whole number; a complete entity. Just like it takes maintenance to ensure the integrity, wholeness, and functionality of a machine, so too does it take maintenance to safeguard the integrity, wholeness, and functionality of an individual.

Are you whole? Are you one? Do you represent yourself as a complete, singular entity? Or do the circumstances of the moment, the event, or the group you're with dictate who you are and how you show up?

Do you maintain your integrity and functional ability? What routines serve as maintenance for your mind, body, and spirit? Do you rest? Do you refuel? Are you in proper working condition?

This third form of integrity is represented by honoring your wholeness. In other words, you are a true and authentic representation of yourself. You maintain your mind, body, and spirit in a healthy and consistent manner. I contend that this form of integrity is the most important of the three in terms of healthy balance. It serves as a foundation for the other two.

For nine consecutive years, I coached youth basketball in the local recreational league. In 2016, I led a team of eleven- and twelve-year-old boys, a very sensitive age when kids become more image conscious. No one wants to look bad. Being cool is important.

With a team of right-handed players, I challenged everyone to learn to shoot left-handed layups. It's a distinct advantage and a necessary skill to advance in the sport. Of course, the majority of the kids looked silly as they attempted their first series of left-handed layups. I reassured them by saying, "Hey, it's practice; no one is watching. Don't worry about what you look like." We repeated this drill at every practice leading up to the first game of the season.

During warm-ups for the first game that year, we started the layup drill from the right side where the kids could use their dominant hand to shoot effective layups. Eventually, I told the kids to switch the layup drill to the left side of the basket. In spite of my prior instructions, most of the kids continued shooting with their right hand from the left side of the basket.

Why?

There was an audience. This was the first game. Family and friends were watching their every move. Grandma was cheering for them from the stands. Even a teacher from school came to watch a few of her grade school boys play.

The kids didn't want to look foolish in front of family and friends. They weren't yet comfortable shooting a layup with their left hand and had no intention of exposing this weakness in their game.

However, in spite of the new sets of eyeballs on my team, there was one kid who repeatedly attempted to shoot with his left hand during the warm-up drill. He looked awkward and didn't come close to making a shot. During the drill, I pulled him aside and let him know that I was so proud that he continued to do the right thing while everyone *was* watching. Eventually, that child became the first one on our team to perfect the left-handed layup.

While the *worth* component of integrity may be defined by what you do when no one is watching, I contend that the *wholeness* component of integrity is more aptly defined by what you do when everyone *is* watching. Are you willing to expose the left hand in the midst of your family, friends, and colleagues? Are you self-aware? Are you genuine in your relationships? Do you accurately represent yourself to the world as an imperfect yet loved human being? Or do you aim to be something you're not, deferring to the perceived expectations and affirmation of others?

Your wholeness is largely defined by your authenticity. If you embrace this broader definition of integrity, you'll simplify your life. You'll rid yourself of the exhausting habit of presenting yourself in a different light to different people. And in establishing or restoring your wholeness, you'll become a leader who's more likely to honor your word and maintain your worth. You'll foster an environment that promotes honesty and ethics and demonstrates it whether others are watching or not.

As a recovering people-pleaser, I can honestly admit that I struggle with this area of integrity the most. I spent far too much time trying to control other's impressions of me. As I think about my childhood, I wonder if I pursued an amateur football career because of my passion for the sport *or* because I thought it portrayed an image that I coveted. Did I accept the first high-paying job I could get because of a passion for business and consulting *or* because others might assume I was successful? Did I pursue an advanced degree in engineering management because I loved systems engineering projects *or* because it added to a resume that reinforced an image of accomplishment?

Are you capable of living a healthy, balanced life if your actions are driven by such superficial motivations? Are you capable of peace if you hide a perceived weakness to gain favor or approval of others? Will you ever be truly fulfilled if you continue to represent yourself as something you're not?

How many stories do we have to hear about someone who's struggled with their sexual identity? For years and even decades, they hide their true self. Our religion, politics, and culture require it. Even our military implemented a policy of "don't ask, don't tell." While some saw this policy as a way to advance the rights of a discriminated population, I can't image anyone affected saw it that way. Imagine being told: "We won't ask about the person you are; and please, for God's sake, don't tell us about the person you are."

Regardless of your view of the issue, consider the implications of these statements on your life. In what areas of your life have you ever felt inferior? Have you been told to *be* a certain way—to change your attire, appearance, or manner of speech? Worse yet, have you ever experienced discrimination for who you are?

Choosing, or being forced to live a disingenuous life is debilitating. You pretend to be someone or something you're not. Whatever the circumstances, hopefully, you're able to accept yourself as you are. From my observation, the sense of relief and freedom is palpable. The individual is stronger, more confident, and better prepared to lead an authentic life. In some cases, the response from those who may not understand or accept the person may be painful or even threatening. Regardless, are you going to live your life in fear of the impression or the affirmation of others? When you live this way, you surrender the CONN to others. You're in the passenger seat of the vehicle you call your life.

 An Important Side Note

> I acknowledge that I may never fully comprehend what it's like to experience discrimination for the color of my skin, heritage of my family, gender that I choose, person that I love, or faith I profess. While I believe authentic ownership of the person that you are is critical to mental and spiritual health, I'm guessing there are circumstances that warrant other considerations beyond my comprehension. It simply pains me to acknowledge that such discrimination persists and that individuals may have compelling reasons to hide the true nature of their being.

In 1974, my parents moved from Anoka, Minnesota, where I was born, to Pittsburgh, Pennsylvania. The move happened a couple weeks before my beloved Pittsburgh Steelers would defeat the Minnesota Vikings in Super Bowl IX, their first of four Super Bowl victories over a six-year span. (As a side note, our house-warming welcome in the North Hills suburb of Pittsburgh was toilet paper in our trees. My parents made the mistake of hanging a large purple invitation to vandalize our house across the garage door of our home.)

As a three-and-a-half-year-old, I don't remember these events. But I do remember an event that happened about two weeks later. Our front yard was on a steep slope as is common in the suburbs of Pittsburgh. One day, after receiving a new blanket of snow, I went outside with my siblings. I was a big boy now. I was going to man my own sled down the new terrain of our front yard.

Like my son nearly thirty-two years later, I sped across our front yard in a rudderless ship. The joy of the experience was cut short as my sled turned unexpectedly, and I slammed head first into the street sign with the poignant and not so ironic notice of "Slow—Children at Play."

All I remember is lying on our kitchen counter with my head under the sink as my mother tried to stop the bleeding and wash my face. In the midst of my frantic cries, I imagine my mother scrambling to prep me for the trip to the emergency room while arranging for a neighbor to watch my brother and sister until my father could get home from work.

Sixteen stitches and two decades later, the physical scar had expanded. A receding hairline threatened to expose what I'd previously hid. I was insecure about what I would look like with a long, jagged scar exposed on the side of my head. What would others think of me?

So, I did what most of us tend to do. I covered it up. I had a procedure done to hide what I feared. What irony. I created a new scar to conceal an old scar.

How often do our efforts to hide old scars create new ones? How often are our actions driven by the anticipated perception or judgment of others as opposed to a true and genuine expression of who we are and who we aren't?

The Bible speaks to this form of integrity as the "Light." John 3:20 says, "Whoever lives by the truth comes into the light. . . ." Acclaimed author and inspirational speaker Brene Brown calls it vulnerability, the courage to be imperfect. Either way, it's living an authentic life of truth without the fear, guilt, or shame of being exposed for who and what you are. It means that you're human. You're the exposed, naked reality of truth. Get comfortable with it.

In your pursuit of healthy balance, you *must* tackle what makes you insecure. What is it that keeps you from living an authentic life? What are you hiding and why? Are you secure with what you know, what you have, and who you are? Such security is required to live an authentic life.

When coaching leaders from the information technology industry, I often refer to cyber security's three-factor authentication, which is considered the gold standard for the protection of information and resources. It provides an apt metaphor as this layered approach to information security includes:

1. What you know (e.g., passwords, PIN, user ID, etc.)
2. What you have (e.g., key fob, access card, digital certificate, etc.)
3. Who you are (e.g., fingerprint, retinal scan, voice recognition, etc.)

While the application of any single factor in isolation provides some measure of security, such an incomplete solution is considered vulnerable. It's the application of all three factors of authentication that provides a near impenetrable level of security.

Just as these three factors of authentication can be applied to protect information and assets, they can also be applied to protect your integrity, personal security, and peace of mind. We refer to this as "3-Factor Authenticity."

1. *What you know*: The first layer of authenticity is self-awareness. What are your strengths and limitations? What do you do well? What are your interests? What are your weaknesses? What has shaped you into the person you are today? What do you value most? Honest reflection and assessment of these questions are necessary to live an authentic life. *Know* the person you are to establish the foundation of true authenticity.

2. *What you have*: The second layer of authenticity is acknowledgment and appreciation of what you have as opposed to what you don't. What are the blessings in your life? These

may include material possessions such as a home or finances. More importantly, this includes the relationships you have and the people you value most. Avoid comparison; it's the enemy of contentment and authenticity. *Own* and appreciate what you have.

3. *Who you are*: The third and final layer of authenticity is how you present yourself to the world. Do you present yourself in a manner that's consistent with what you know about yourself and what you have? Or, do you attempt to present yourself as something or someone you're not or that you wish to be? Worse yet, is your *who* circumstantial depending on the people you're with or where you are? *Be* the person you mean to be in order to live a life of true peace and integrity.

I encourage you to practice and embrace all three forms of authenticity in your life. Take an inventory of the person you are as opposed to who you pretend to be. Note the gaps. Observe the impact your insecurities have on your relationships and your life. It's through the combined application of these principles that any individual can pursue a life of integrity, personal security, fulfillment, and peace. *Know It, Own It, Be It . . . CEEK a Better Way.*

 Journal – Questions to Consider

- Where in my life do I present myself as something or someone other than who I truly am?
- How does this impact my relationships and feelings of self-worth?
- What warning signs exist and guardrails can I adopt to better honor my wholeness?

 Exercise – Consider a Deeper Dive

Identify up to three instances where you've presented yourself in an inauthentic manner. Honestly assess your motivation for the inauthentic behavior. Document how this observation makes you feel. What impact did it have on your self-worth and general peace? Pinpoint three actions you can take or other actions you can stop that will help you to be more authentic and whole at work and in life. Practice these actions and note the impact.

CHAPTER 14

LAUGH

As soap is to the body, so laughter is to the soul.

~ Jewish Proverb

Close this book. Watch a funny show, share a funny story, call that funny friend. Laugh.

CHAPTER 15

DISCOVER PEACE

Our life is two dates with a dash in the middle.
What are you going to do with that dash?

~ Attributed to Stuart Scott

I started CEEK LLC in 2013. As an aspiring business owner without a brick and mortar store, I worked anywhere and everywhere. With a daughter who spends many hours per week perfecting her craft, I often parked myself in the lobby of her gymnastics club. Rather than drive back and forth, I found it was a convenient way to get work done with only the occasional interruptions to watch nervously as my daughter worked on new skills.

So, there I was in July of 2014, drafting a blog post for the new CEEK website. It was my first post tackling the subject of healthy balance. I was experiencing writer's block, so I decided to take a break. I went to the window overlooking the gym. There my daughter stood on a narrow wooden rail that is sixteen feet long and four inches wide. She leaped into the air and flipped backward. As her right foot landed squarely on the beam, her left foot grazed the side, and my daughter tumbled to the ground. She gathered herself and pulled herself back up onto the beam.

After a couple deep breaths, she again leaped into the air, tucked her legs, and tumbled backward. This time her left foot followed the lead of the right foot. She landed squarely in the center of the beam. She glanced at the window and smiled before repeating the skill a couple more times.

After my heart began beating again, I returned to my seat in sheer awe of the strength, flexibility, balance, skill, and courage it must take to execute such a maneuver successfully. As I woke my computer from its slumber, I heard the familiar ding of an incoming email. It was a message from a friend sending an embedded video link.

I clicked the link, sat back, and watched for the next three minutes and fifty-two seconds. The video began with a bald man about my age, standing on a narrow wooden plank sixteen feet long and four inches wide. The man's name was Francis Chan. He briefly mentioned a few facts of his life: his mother died during his birth, his stepmom died in a car accident when he was nine, and his father died of cancer when he was twelve. After a few years under the care of an aunt and uncle, his new parents had an argument. His uncle shot his aunt before turning the gun on himself.

By age sixteen, Francis had lived a shaky, unbalanced life. However, he refused to be a victim. He took the CONN. Francis built and sustained a strong faith foundation in spite of the adversity he'd faced. He pursued a master of divinity degree, founded a church in California, authored multiple best-selling books, and led various businesses that he used to fund mission work across the world. The video had more than one million views at that time.

In the video, Francis was standing on the beam just as my daughter had minutes earlier. Only he performed a much simpler routine. He described our propensity to play it safe when life throws adversity our way. When we're overcome by fear and anxiety, he demonstrated how we crouch down and hug the beam. We're afraid to fail, afraid to fall, afraid to take a risk and live our life to the fullest. He ended his routine with a slow and cautious dismount. He capped off the metaphor with an Olympic-style salute before God in recognition of the life he had been blessed to live.

As Stuart Scott said, what are you going to do with your dash? If that "dash" were sixteen feet long and four inches wide, would you hug it tightly for the rest of your life? Are you content to be among the two-thirds of the workforce going through the motions as a disengaged zombie? Will you continue to blame others for your lack of balance, fulfillment, and peace, all the while surrendering the CONN to your boss, your spouse, your colleagues, your kids, or the socioeconomic and political circumstances of the moment? Or will you, like my daughter, take a risk, fall, and get back up? Will you get in the game? Are you willing to tumble and fall?

Stand up on the dash that is your life! Risk your balance to restore it. Fall. Get up. Perfect your routine.

I'm a recovering victim who blamed others for my lack of balance and fulfillment. Several years ago, I chose to get back in the game. I took control of my life. I stood up on my dash with a fully exposed set of values and a compelling mission. I practiced and perfected my routine, consistent with the priorities and skills I desired for my life. I fell. I got back up. I took big risks and perfected new skills.

You've reached the end of PART II, which has offered a proven approach to help you discover healthy balance.

- **Pursue a values-based mission.** Assess your core values and identify a compelling purpose. Determine the associated life priorities and define *balance* in light of those priorities. Discover and apply creative ways to connect your purpose with your career or life's work.

- **Establish routines.** State daily, weekly, monthly, and yearly routines in support of the priorities of your life. Enrich such routines with an "ePIC" expression of your values. Don't sacrifice the important for the perpetually urgent. Build in accountability.

- **Appreciate the moment.** Enhance your awareness of the thoughts that command your attention. Establish the discipline to become more mindful. Replace negative thoughts with positive affirmations. Learn to put the balls down and live in the moment.

- **Choose your disposition.** Observe your reactions to people, places, things, and circumstances. Assess how those reactions impact your general disposition. *"Take the CONN"* opting for a better response. Build a new habit. Choose dispositional optimism and confirm it daily.

- Embrace a broader integrity. Recognize that integrity is more than honesty and ethics and honoring your word. Pursue wholeness of mind, body, and spirit. Put in place the guardrails necessary to protect and sustain your integrity. Embrace vulnerability and lead an authentic life.

As the acronym of these five steps suggests, it is through the pursuit of healthy life balance that you will discover PEACE. This isn't the type of peace that reflects the absence of conflict or war. This peace frees you from fear and anxiety. It relieves you of the tendency to compare and judge. It provides the tranquility of knowing that you're living without regret. You're whole. You're comfortable and at ease living a life consistent with what you know, what you have, and who you are. And when you face adversity and conflict, you now have the tools to move through it with PEACE.

And by all means, please don't simply make the recommended list of activities in this book yet another excuse that perpetuates your life as a human doing as opposed to a human being. Intermixed with the core chapters of this book are five reminders of your humanity. Take the time to BREATHE, WALK, REST, PLAY, and LAUGH. Honor the space between the notes.

You now know what to do. Keep in mind that average people know what to do.

Exceptional people *do what they know.*

> **P**ursue a values-based mission.
> **E**stablish routines.
> **A**ppreciate the moment.
> **C**hoose your disposition.
> **E**mbrace a broader integrity.

CEEK . . . a Better Way!

Journal – Questions to Consider

- What am I going to do with my dash?
- How do I now define life balance?
- What does PEACE mean to me in my life?

 Exercise – Consider a Deeper Dive

In your journal, describe your dash to this point in your life. Summarize how you've lived your life thus far relative to your mission, values, and professed priorities. Identify what you're most proud of. Express any fears and regrets that linger. Based on what you've discovered through this book and the associated exercises, describe the remainder of the dash that represents your life. What will be different? How will you be remembered? What impact will you have? How do you define the PEACE of a life well lived? Believe it before you see it . . . then *"Take the CONN!"*

Share the Adventure

*If you have an apple and I have an apple and we exchange
these apples, then you and I will still each have one
apple. But if you have an idea and I have an idea and we
exchange these ideas, then each of us will have two ideas.*

~ George Bernard Shaw

Through this book, I have shared my doubts, fears, insecurities, failures, discoveries, aspirations, and triumphs in my pursuit of healthy balance, personal fulfillment, and professional success. My hope is that you were able to relate to some aspects of my story in a way that helps you in your journey.

If my stories, life experiences, failures, and successes were of value to you, consider for a moment that your stories, life experiences, failures, and successes may be valuable to others. In the spirit of George Bernard Shaw's quote, I encourage you to share your adventure. It's through shared ideas and knowledge that we can exponentially transform the minds of individuals and the culture of organizations in a way that promotes personal fulfillment and professional success. That is the very intention of this book.

One of the best and most productive ways to share ideas and knowledge to the benefit of yourself and others is by engaging a small group of trusted friends and colleagues to participate in this journey together. Just as vacations can be more fun and memorable with people you love, so too can the journey inward be more enlightening and meaningful when you bring others along with you. The journey to the authentic self can be difficult. Yet, when it's done in the company of others whom you trust enough to be vulnerable in front of, the learning can be exponentially greater, the realizations fundamentally deeper.

Even if you have already "completed" the questions and activities suggested throughout this book, I encourage you to engage a study group of friends or colleagues as a means to better understand the material in this book. Finding others who share your innate curiosity can enable the group to plumb the depths of issues and collectively lift everyone to greater heights of understanding.

Here are some suggestions on how to get a study group started and what to expect:

1. Recruit up to six people for this group but no more so that everyone has a chance to participate in each meeting. (Fewer people is fine, too.)
2. As a group, decide on a timeframe for completing the book together. Be sure to give everyone sufficient time to read the chapters, answer the questions, and do the deeper-dive activities.
3. Meet on a recurring basis to discuss what you learned from each chapter and to share insights, lessons, and observations regarding the questions to consider and deeper-dive activities.

The critical component of this group is *listening*. The point is to share your findings with the group and listen to the others as they share. Learning comes by listening to what others bring and incorporating what makes sense into your psyche. Discussions are encouraged. Just remember that no one is in the group to *fix* someone else. That behavior is strongly *discouraged*.

Understand that someone might drop out. It happens. The goal is to be kind, understanding, and reflective. There's no one right way to do this process. Allow the group to develop a flow of its own in your collective efforts to *CEEK a Better Way*.

Acknowledgments

As a husband and father, business owner, volunteer, and now author, I learned an ironic lesson over the course of the yearlong effort to write and publish this book. It's difficult to sustain healthy life balance while writing a book about the pursuit of healthy life balance. Fortunately, I have many people in my life who helped me do just that.

First, I thank my wife for giving me the space, patience, and support to pursue this initiative in the midst of our already busy schedules. More importantly, I thank you for your gentle touch over the years to help me discover and address my own struggles with balance while you served as the rock for our family. Your unconditional love and support make me a better person.

We are blessed to have two remarkable children. I thank you both for the joy you bring to our lives. Your heart, humor, and humility are evident in the way you carry yourself at school, in the gym, on the field, at home, and in the world. Your influence on this book should be evident throughout. I hope you find it a useful tool as you navigate your own professional and life aspirations. Your potential is unlimited.

I'm very fortunate to have grown up with the influence and support of a remarkable family. I thank my mother for teaching me countless life lessons, demonstrating the importance of compassion, understanding, and empathy for others. I thank my father for showing me the value of hard work and discipline balanced with a remarkable ability to simply "just be" with others. To my brother, you've always been an extraordinary role model and source of wisdom in all aspects of life. Anyone would be fortunate to have such an example. And to my sister, you're the defender of all that is good. Thank you for your friendship, influence, and feedback throughout my life and throughout the development of this book, in particular.

In addition to my own family, I greatly value and appreciate my new CEEK family as we share the vision to rid the world of zombies in the workforce. Jennifer Hughes, Abby Allen, Whitley Carson, Kristen Gauthier, and Chris King, thank you for embracing our mission together and pushing me to put my words on paper. This book wouldn't have happened without your collective influence.

In particular, I thank Jennifer for the loyalty, friendship, and support that has shaped this book in ways you may never fully understand. Like you do for your clients, you inspire me to achieve what I didn't think was achievable. Whitley, thank you for your creative genius. In addition to the cover design, your influence has permeated all aspects of design and marketing. Kristen, many thanks for the most thorough review of the book from anyone that reviewed early drafts. I hope it's clear to you the influence your perspective has had on this final version.

I'd also be remiss not to thank the two youngest members of the CEEK team. As a college intern, I thank Madison Wright for developing the *Life Balance Assessment* that accompanies this book. And, another special thank you to my daughter, who researched all the sources referenced throughout the book and prepared the list of references. It's been a pleasure working with the next generation of professional leaders.

There have been countless other individuals and organizations that have had a tremendous influence on my life and in the content of this book. Unfortunately, there are too many to list here. However, I would like to thank the Crosspointe Church community as a whole and Jonathan Bow and Steve Daugherty specifically. Your teachings have had a tremendous influence on the spiritual foundation of my family and me. Such influence should be evident throughout the pages of this book. Furthermore, through your innovative leadership, our community built a YMCA on the grounds of our church with an atrium and coffee shop bridging Crosspointe to the YMCA. It was there that I was often found working on this book. Thank you for the inspiration, love, and support.

I'd also like to thank the early reviewers of my book. I've been influenced from afar by Chalmers Brothers and his book, *Language and the Pursuit of Happiness*. Dianne Falk offers the perspective of a former executive and now leadership coach who has successfully navigated family and career. My college friend and teammate, Todd Durkin, has inspired me and millions of others through his books, motivational engagements, and physical, mental, and spiritual coaching. And Cathy Fenwick is a young mother of three, balancing family with a promising career as president of Harmonics Consulting. Samples of the feedback from these individuals can be found on the back cover of this book. I thank you all for the feedback and validation of the need for this book.

I'm grateful to Kristine Sisson, the author of the foreword. I'm inspired by your story and willingness to openly share the details of your journey. I greatly value our shared experience and, in spite of time and distance, consider you a valued friend.

I'd like to thank Diana M. Needham and the team of consultants she brought to assist me in this endeavor. As a proven Book Shepherd, Diana guided me through the process from an idea in my head to words on paper and finally to this book in your hands. I thank you for the guidance, encouragement, and coaching throughout. In particular, I also appreciate the introduction to Lisbeth Tanz, the editor of this book. I thank you, Lis, for the thorough review and honest insights and feedback. I've learned a great deal from your efforts and have no doubt of the impact you had in improving the quality, applicability, and readability of this finished product.

Lastly, I thank countless other friends and colleagues who have openly shared their stories with me. It's reassuring to know that we're not alone in our struggles to discover and sustain healthy life balance. I thank you all for the collective influence and support.

Appendix of Questions and Exercises

Throughout this book, I have included questions for reflection and suggested exercises to reinforce the concepts shared within each of the chapters. This appendix provides a summary of all of the questions and exercises posed by chapter and section within each chapter. As my free gift to you, you can also access a workbook with these questions and exercises as well as CEEK's Life Balance Assessment from the following site, accessible only to those who purchased *Navigate Chaos*: www.ceekllc.com/balance. This assessment will enable you to assess the priorities in your life and provide valuable insights as you answer the questions and complete the activities listed below.

CHAPTER 4: THE DISCOVERY

Realities

- In what aspects of your life are professed priorities inconsistent with your demonstrated behaviors?
- What warning signs exist that you're falling or headed for a fall?
- In what aspects of your life do you need to refuel or "sharpen the saw?"
- What warning signs exist that you're running out of gas?
- In what areas of your life does overuse come at the expense of other priorities?
- What warning signs can you see of impending mental, physical, or spiritual injury?

Myths

- How do you define healthy life balance?
- Are you mentally, physically, and spiritually prepared for the *next* unanticipated event or adversity?

- How might the effective pursuit of life balance enhance your productivity and professional success?

CHAPTER 5: PURSUE *A* MISSION

State your values and purpose

Journal – Questions to Consider

- Whom do I admire most?
- What breaks my heart?
- What do these responses reveal about my core values?

Exercise – Consider a Deeper Dive

In your journal, respond to the questions to consider and note the words, concepts, or ideas that resonate most as core values that you hold. Identify three to five values that best describe you and what you care about most deeply. Draft a personal mission statement that inspires you in a manner consistent with these values and what you care about. Write it down. Share it with others. Commit to reassess and revise this statement as necessary. Refer to this statement and your core values as you complete the other activities suggested throughout this book.

Define balance in light of your priorities

Journal – Questions to Consider

- Considering my mission and core values, what are the priorities in my life (e.g., family, faith, career, health, e.g.)?
- How do my demonstrated behaviors—how I live my life—align with or differ from my professed priorities?
- How have my priorities changed over time?

Exercise – Consider a Deeper Dive

Complete the *CEEK Life Balance Assessment* (www.ceekllc.com/balance). Use the results of the assessment to define what balance means to you in terms of your commitment to the professed priorities of your life. Note your observations in your journal.

Connect your purpose to your work

Journal – Questions to Consider

- How can I redesign my job to better align my work with my newly defined mission and/or values?
- What actions can I take to demonstrate this alignment with my mission and/or values?
- Who must I engage with and what conversations or steps must I take to facilitate the necessary changes?

Exercise – Consider a Deeper Dive

Rewrite your job description in a way that connects to your personal mission statement and values. Consider defining your job in terms of *why* as opposed to *what* you do. Determine how this will change how you approach your work. Identify the rituals you can put in place that become your *signature* or what you are known for in your profession.

CHAPTER 7: ESTABLISH ROUTINES

Specify recurring rituals

Journal – Questions to Consider

- What current activities in my life demonstrate a commitment to the life priorities I have identified?
- What new recurring activities would help further reinforce the professed priorities of my life?
- How might a commitment to such activities support my mental, physical, or spiritual well-being?

Exercise – Consider a Deeper Dive

For each of the *Life Balance Tensions* identified in your *CEEK Life Balance Assessment*, define at least four goals, stated as daily, weekly, monthly, or yearly commitments, that you can make to reinforce your professed priorities in life. Specify the schedule and frequency with which you commit to fulfilling each activity. As appropriate, place the specified commitments on your home and work calendars. Track your progress as a relative percentage of commitments maintained. Note your progress in your journal.

Express your values

Journal – Questions to Consider

- What behaviors or rituals can I adopt as a personal expression of the mission and values I've defined?
- Where and how can I apply these behaviors or rituals in my life?
- How will the persistent application of these behaviors or rituals over time make me feel?

Exercise – Consider a Deeper Dive

Think of three people in your life whom you remember because of a unique and impactful behavior, greeting, mantra, etc., that they exhibited over an extended period of time. In your journal, document your thoughts about the values each person revealed through their repeated behavior. Now, revisit your mission and core values. Assess if your mission and values are visible to your family, friends, and colleagues through your behaviors or rituals. Identify at least one differentiating behavior or ritual that you'll adopt as a reflection of your values. Try it out for three weeks, and observe how it makes you and others feel.

Sustain what is important

Journal – Questions to Consider

Refer to your core values and the behaviors or activities that you identified to support the priorities in your life.

- In what aspects of my life do I sacrifice my values or life priorities for the perpetually urgent?
- How do such actions, or inaction, affect me mentally, physically, or spiritually?
- What actions can I take to hold myself accountable to the activities and rituals that reinforce my priorities?

Exercise – Consider a Deeper Dive

Identify a time that you sacrificed a personal value for an urgent demand. Describe the circumstances of the event. What did you do? How did you rationalize it in your mind? How did your actions make you feel in retrospect? If you had to do it all over again, what would you have done differently? Note these observations in your journal.

For each of the daily, weekly, monthly, and yearly commitments you identified earlier to support priorities in your life, define specifics to hold yourself accountable. In your journal, note the frequency, timeframe, and resources needed to fulfill the obligation. List the actions you can take or people you can engage to hold you accountable.

CHAPTER 9: APPRECIATE THE MOMENT

Become more mindful

Journal – Questions to Consider

- What sources of information do I consume on a regular basis?
- How does the repetitive consumption of this information influence my thoughts throughout each day?
- How do such thoughts impact the demonstration of my defined values and professed priorities?

Exercise – Consider a Deeper Dive

Make a list of those things that you consume or that influence your thoughts on a recurring basis (music, media, news, people, places, circumstances, and other things). Observe and note in your journal the impact those things have on your thoughts, mood, and energy. Build awareness. Mentally commit to acknowledging the thoughts that arise when you experience these things. Don't judge these thoughts. Simply acknowledge them and write down your observations.

Put the balls down

Journal – Questions to Consider

- What *ball* do I carry with me most often?
- How does this tendency affect my joy or appreciation of the other priorities in my life?
- What warning signs exist that I'm carrying too many balls at once?

Exercise – Consider a Deeper Dive

Define a mental exercise (e.g., a mantra, self-reminder, meditation, etc.) to symbolically put down any balls that impose on the activities you identified in support of other life priorities. Practice this mental exercise over the course of three weeks. Observe and write down in your journal the impact of this exercise on your focus, productivity, relationships, and general fulfillment.

Live in the moment

Journal – Questions to Consider

- Under what circumstances (where, when, and how often) do I find myself mentally distracted from conversations, tasks, or other activities?
- How do these distractions affect my general productivity?
- How do these distractions affect my relationships?

Exercise – Consider a Deeper Dive

Write about a recent scenario in which you weren't fully present in the moment. Describe the impact that your lack of focused attention or appreciation of the moment had on your productivity or a relationship. Alternatively, identify a recent scenario in which you were fully present in the moment. Similarly, describe the effect of focused attention on your productivity, relationship, and personal fulfillment. Decide on three things you can do physically (e.g., put the cell phone away, move to a new space, etc.) or mentally (e.g., additional mantra, meditation, etc.) to enhance your presence in the activities that will reinforce your life priorities and the most important relationships in your life.

CHAPTER 11: CHOOSE YOUR DISPOSITION

Observe your reactions

Journal – Questions to Consider

- What people, places, things, or circumstances generate positive or negative reactions in me?
- What is the reason or underlying motivation for my reactions?
- How do such reactions help or hinder me?

Exercise – Consider a Deeper Dive

Spend two weeks noting your reactions to people, places, things, or circumstances that generate strong emotions, positive and negative. Describe the circumstances in your journal, and write your rationale for your reaction. Don't judge your reactions. Simply acknowledge them and write down your observations.

Assess your disposition

Journal – Questions to Consider

- How do the people, places, things, or circumstances that generate undesirable reactions color my general mood or disposition?
- How do these circumstances impact my tendency toward dispositional optimism or pessimism?
- How do such circumstances affect how I show up in the priority areas of my life?

Exercise – Consider a Deeper Dive

Return to the list of activities or routines you defined for the priority areas of your life. For each activity or routine, consider the impact that your general disposition has on your appreciation of the priority and the activity. Note these observations in your journal.

Take the CONN

Journal – Questions to Consider

- How do I generally show up in the world? How would I like to show up in the world?
- Using your list of people, places, things, or circumstances that generate negative reactions, ask: What is a better, alternative reaction to such circumstances?
- What can I do to build a new habit in how I respond?

Exercise – Consider a Deeper Dive

Select three of the most common circumstances that cause an undesired reaction. For each, plan an alternative response. Practice the response for three weeks and note the impact on your general mood and disposition, as well as the impact on your participation in the activities and routines that reinforce the priorities in your life. Record your thoughts in your journal, including any perceived impact on your productivity, balance, relationships, and general fulfillment.

CHAPTER 13: EMBRACE A BROADER INTEGRITY

Honor your worth

Journal – Questions to Consider

- How have small lapses of judgment led to bigger transgressions in my life?
- Where in my life might my honesty and ethics be tested?
- What guardrails can I adopt to honor my worth?

Exercise – Consider a Deeper Dive

Identify three instances from your experience and relationships where people were exposed for unethical behavior. What circumstances led to these behaviors. (If you don't know, imagine what circumstances may have led to them.) Identify a point at which the individual could have or should have drawn the line or put a stop to the sequence of events that led to the unethical behavior. Identify and commit to three guardrails that will protect you from a series of events that could lead to similar circumstances. Apply these guardrails and note the impact.

Honor your word

Journal – Questions to Consider

- How clear are the requests that I receive and make?
- Where in my life do I overcommit? What are the reasons that I make such commitments?
- What filters and behaviors can I adopt to better honor my word?

Exercise – Consider a Deeper Dive

Identify three instances where you failed to follow through on a commitment. Assess the circumstances that contributed to both making the commitment and not following through. Were the request and eventual commitment clear? Identify what you would have done differently in retrospect. Document and practice three controls you can put in place to avoid making unreasonable commitments. Also, consider how you can better respond if and when you do miss a commitment. Practice these controls and note the impact.

Honor your wholeness

Journal – Questions to Consider

- Where in my life do I present myself as something or someone other than who I truly am?
- How does this impact my relationships and feelings of self-worth?
- What warning signs exist and guardrails can I adopt to better honor my wholeness?

Exercise – Consider a Deeper Dive

Identify up to three instances where you've presented yourself in an inauthentic manner. Honestly assess your motivation for the inauthentic behavior. Document how this observation makes you feel. What impact did it have on your self-worth and general peace? Pinpoint three actions you can take or other actions you can stop that will help you to be more authentic and whole at work and in life. Practice these actions and note the impact.

CHAPTER 15: DISCOVER PEACE

Journal – Questions to Consider

- What am I going to do with my dash?
- How do I now define life balance?
- What does PEACE mean to me in my life?

Exercise – Consider a Deeper Dive

In your journal, describe your dash to this point in your life. Summarize how you've lived your life thus far relative to your mission, values, and professed priorities. Identify what you're most proud of. Express any fear and regrets that linger. Based on what you've discovered through this book and the associated exercises, describe the remainder of the dash that represents your life. What will be different? How will you be remembered? What impact will you have? How do you define the PEACE of a life well lived? Believe it before you see it ... then *"Take the CONN!"*

References

Part I

Chapter 4:

Brothers, C. (2005). *Language and the Pursuit of Happiness: A New Foundation for Designing Your Life, Your Relationships & Your Results*. Naples, FL: New Possibilities Press.

Covey, S. R. (2004). *The 7 Habits of Highly Effective People: Powerful Lessons in Personal Change*. New York, NY: Free Press.

Mandela, N. (1995). *Long Walk to Freedom: The Autobiography of Nelson Mandela*. New York, NY: Back Bay Books.

Reider, B. (2017). "Too Much? Too Soon?" *The American Journal of Sports Medicine*, 45(6), 1249-1251. https://doi.org/10.1177/0363546517705349

Part II

Sharma, R. (2011). *The Monk Who Sold His Ferrari: A Remarkable Story About Living Your Dreams*. New York, NY: HarperCollins Publishers.

Chapter 5:

Gallup. (2017). *State of the American Workplace* (3rd ed.). Washington, D.C.: Gallup.

Leipzig, A. (2013, Feb 1). "How to Know Your Life Purpose in 5 Minutes" [Video File]. Retrieved from https://www.youtube.com/watch?v=vVsXO9brK7M

Lencioni, P. M. (2008). *The Three Big Questions for a Frantic Family: A Leadership Fable About Restoring Sanity to the Most Important Organization in Your Life*. San Francisco, CA: Jossey-Bass.

Wrzesniewski, A., Berg, J.M., & Dutton, J. E. (2010). "Turn the job you have into the job you want." *Harvard Business Review,* 88(6), 114-117.

Wrzesniewski, A. [re:Work with Google]. (2014, Nov. 10). *Job Crafting – Amy Wrzesniewski on Creating Meaning in Your Own Work* [Video File]. Retrieved from https://www.youtube.com/watch?v=C_igfnctYjA.

Chapter 7:

Lewis, M. (2016). *The Undoing Project: A Friendship That Changed Our Minds.* New York, NY: W. W. Norton & Company.

Chapter 9:

Manion, J. (2014). *Satisfied: Discovering Contentment in a World of Consumption.* Grand Rapids, MI: Zondervan.

Ward, A. F., Duke, K., Gneezy, A. & Bos, M. W. (2017). "Brain Drain: The Mere Presence of One's Own Smartphone Reduces Available Cognitive Capacity" [Abstract]. *Journal for the Association for Consumer Research* 2(2), 140–154.

Chapter 11:

Brothers, C. (2005). *Language and the Pursuit of Happiness: A New Foundation for Designing Your Life, Your Relationships & Your Results.* Naples, FL: New Possibilities Press.

Pausch, R., & Zaslow, J. (2008). *The Last Lecture.* London: Hachette Books.

Seligman, M. (2011). *Learned Optimism: How to Change Your Mind and Your Life.* New York, NY: Vintage Books.

Villarica, H. (2012). "How the Power of Positive Thinking Won Scientific Credibility." *The Atlantic.* Retrieved from https://www.theatlantic.com/health/archive/2012/04/how-the-power-of-positive-thinking-won-scientific-credibility/256223/ https://dammitdolls.com/Home

Chapter 13:

Brothers, C. (2005). *Language and the Pursuit of Happiness: A New Foundation for Designing Your Life, Your Relationships & Your Results*. Naples, FL: New Possibilities Press.

Krakauer, J. (2015). *Missoula: Rape and the Justice System in a College Town*. New York: Doubleday.

Ford, B. D. (2011, Oct. 23). "Joe Papp's Long and Winding Road." ESPN. Retrieved from http://www.espn.com/espn/otl/story/_/id/7132452/former-cyclist-joe-papp-gets-three-years-probation-ped-case

Sharma, R. (2011). *The Monk Who Sold His Ferrari: A Remarkable Story About Living Your Dreams*. New York, NY: HarperCollins Publishers.

Chapter 15:

Chan, F. [Posted by golfguy2117]. (2008, Oct. 2). *Francis Chan – Balance Beam* [Video File]. Retrieved from https://www.youtube.com/watch?v=LA_uwWPE6lQ

Scott, S., & Platt, L. (2016). *Every Day I Fight*. New York, NY: Penguin Publishing Group.

About the Author

In the midst of a promising consulting career, Steve Wiley fell in love, bought a new home, and had two children. Although he checked all the boxes for what he thought would be a happy and fulfilling life, he was stressed, exhausted, and unhealthy. Eventually, he crashed. Steve needed a better way to live and work. He intentionally restored the priorities in his life and pursued healthy balance.

After the most successful years of his career and life, he started CEEK LLC with the intention of ridding the world of "zombies" in the workforce. Today, Steve is a successful business owner, author, and inspirational speaker on topics related to culture, values, leadership, and life balance. More importantly, Steve is a fully engaged and loving husband, father, son, brother, friend, and colleague living a healthy, balanced life.

Connect with Steve on LinkedIn: https://www.linkedin.com/in/stwiley

Follow Steve on Twitter: @wileysteven or @ceekllc

Follow Steve on Instagram: @stevenbrettwiley

Visit Steve at CEEK LLC: www.ceekllc.com